Daniel Huntington, *Philosophy and Christian Art.* (1868)
Los Angeles County Museum of Art:
Gift of Will Richeson

CHRISTIAN REVELATION AND THE COMPLETION OF THE ARISTOTELIAN REVOLUTION

Patrick Madigan, S.J.

UNIVERSITY
PRESS OF
AMERICA

Lanham • New York • London

Copyright © 1988 by

University Press of America,® Inc.

4720 Boston Way
Lanham, MD 20706

3 Henrietta Street
London WC2E 8LU England

Printed in the United States of America

British Cataloging in Publication Information Available

Library of Congress Cataloging-in-Publication Data

Madigan, Patrick.
Christian revelation and the completion of the Aristotelian
revolution / Patrick Madigan.
p. cm.
Includes bibliographies.
1. Aristotle—Contributions in metaphysics. 2. Philosophy and
religion—History. 3. Metaphysics—History. 4. Christianity—
Philosophy. I. Title.
B491.M4M33   1988
185—dc 19   88–18663 CIP
ISBN 0–8191–7090–9 (alk. paper)
ISBN 0–8191–7091–7 (pbk. : alk. paper)

All University Press of America books are produced on acid-free paper.
The paper used in this publication meets the minimum requirements of American
National Standard for Information Sciences—Permanence of Paper for Printed
Library Materials, ANSI Z39.48–1984.

. . . We assume that the gods are in the highest degree blessed and happy. But what kind of actions are we to attribute to them? . . . Now, if we take away action from a living being, to say nothing of production, what is left except contemplation?

Aristotle
NICOMACHEAN ETHICS

. . . You brought in my way by means of a certain man . . . some books of the Platonists translated from Greek into Latin. In them I found, though not in the very words, yet the thing itself and proved by all sorts of reasons, that "In the beginning was the Word and the Word was with God and the Word was God . . . all things were made by Him." But I did not read in those books that "He came unto His own" . . . I did not find that "the Word became flesh."

Aurelius Augustinus
THE CONFESSIONS

. . . It pertains to a perfect agent to act by virtue of love for what it possesses, and for this reason (Dionysius) adds that the beautiful that is God is the efficient, moving, and containing cause, "by a love of His own Beauty." Since He has His own Beauty, He wishes to multiply it as far as possible, that is to say, by the communication of His likeness.

Thomas Aquinas
EXPOSITION OF DIONYSIUS ON THE DIVINE NAMES

TABLE OF CONTENTS

PROLOGUE

"Of the making of books, there is no end." So says the book of **Ecclestiastes**, and concerning Aristotle this saying is certainly true. The research continues apace. Those interested in following the stages in the debate over the evolution of the text of Aristotle's **Metaphysics** may consult with profit the 104 brief notices included in Giovanni Reale's masterwork **The Concept of First Philosophy and the Unity of the Metaphysics of Aristotle** (State University of N.Y. Pr., Albany, 1980, tr. Catan). Articles on Aristotle's understanding of science, metaphysics, ethics, and politics have been collected recently by Barnes, Scofield, and Sorabji in their three-volume work (St. Martins Pr., N.Y., 1978). G.E.L. Owen has brought together the papers from a very interesting conference on Aristotle held in 1957 (Goteborg, Sweden, 1960), and Amelie Rorty has presented a group of provocative perspectives and questions generated by the **Ethics** (Berkeley, 1983). In this work I propose to follow modestly in the footsteps of Giovanni Reale and Joseph Owens, in seeing a unity (if also an incompletely fulfilled project) in the texts we have of the **Metaphysics**. In this I believe I am in accord with the majority of contemporary scholars, who have become disenchanted with Werner Jaeger's thesis of 1934 that Aristotle began as a speculative Platonist and ended as an empiricist, in the modern (sceptical) sense, and that this trajectory is to be found sedimented in the various layers of the **Meta-physics**. (If anything, the evidence now seems to suggest a reverse development, of rebellion against and subsequent return to Plato.[1]) Jaeger's thesis is now somewhat dated, and so the distancing of myself from it may be considered non-controversial. Where I propose to make a contribution is in stepping back and addressing a larger issue that seldom comes into focus in monographs on Aristotle, but which nevertheless undergirds and controls, if only through one's choice of vocabulary, the perspective from which studies of Aristotle, and on the relationship between Greek and Medieval philosophy as a whole, continue occasionally to be produced.

I wish to develop a suggestion made by Joseph Owens to the effect that Aristotle's **Metaphysics** is essentially incomplete.[2] That is, what we have in the texts of the **Metaphysics** is a program imperfectly carried out, and this failure is not simply accidental; rather, it is systematic, or due to

1

internal causes. The program could not be carried to completion, in principle. It is not that Aristotle was lazy, nor are we lacking any texts that Aristotle provided originally and which have since become lost. There never were any such texts, they could not have been written. The system does not work now because it did not work then, it has never "worked." Thus this incompleteness can be described as systematic or essential. Starting from this suggestion by Owens, I wish to expand the discussion into an historical perspective in suggesting that it was the spreading influence of the movements of Judaism and Christianity, and the altered view of God they entailed, which supplied (in spite of its philosophically scandalous character) the missing element that the Aristotelian project needed to complete its program. I need not note that this is an historical and systematic thesis which can be studied and evaluated independently of one's stand on the theological claims of Judaism or Christianity. I will argue, specifically, that the spreading movements of Judaism and Christianity interacted with the received Platonic (and later Aristotelian) notions of God in such a way as to allow the general philosophic (and specifically Aristotelian) project (to generate an adequate explanation of the world) to move finally and for the first time towards a serious conclusion; they opened the door to a termination that before was not possible. With the alteration of the Greek notion of God, the internal reason for the essential incompleteness of the Aristotelian system was taken away, the self-imposed impediment was removed, and the road ahead now became clear. In a sense it is an historical accident that Judaism and Christianity performed this role; any religion with a non-mytholigical yet "activist" view of God could have performed the same function (although this excludes Hinduism and Buddhism; the first because it is frankly mythological, the second because of its non-activist view of God). This thesis may appear controversial, however, because it runs counter to the position frequently presented since the Enlightenment, which is that Christianity appropriated, distorted, and perverted the patrimony of Greek philosophy to its own (foreign) purposes, that Christianity weakened, dismembered, or pushed aside the autonomous and free-standing structure that was Greek philosophy, reducing and transforming it into a pillar within its own cathedral. The data now seem to suggest - as they do with Jaeger's provocative thesis about the evolution of the Aristotelian texts - that this thesis is precisely the opposite of what actually happened.

Christianity did not present itself originally as a philosophical system; and indeed, it did make significant borrowings from the received philosophic traditions to express its claims about the messiahship of Jesus - including Stoicism, Platonism, and what since the nineteenth century has been called "Neo-Platonism" (as did also first-century Judaism about the relationship between God and the Torah). However, the fact that no philosophical school managed to command the Greek mind during the Hellenistic period suggests a loss of confidence in the lofty earlier project to construct an adequate explanation of the world, and a consequent lowering of attention to aspects of existence that were, if more immediate and banal, still stubbornly real; further, as increasingly precarious, threatened, and less stable, these conditions of existence were for that reason increasingly important to study, shore up, and if possible guarantee. Christian rhetoric and apologetic first made use of Stoic, but especially Platonic motifs and categories; Jewish and Christian thinkers found Plato's notion of a naturally diffusive "Good" compatible with and suggestive of their notion of a creative God. In this sense, Plato's "revolt" against Parmenides, all the while respecting his central insight, can be described as successfully carried through and brought to one kind of completion in Judaism and Christianity; for if creation is a *necessary* process, and not the result of a separate act on God's part, then the world is not truly distinct from God, and Plato's position collapses back into a variation of Parmenides'. On the other hand, Parmenides reemerges clammoring for his rights in Aristotle, for according to Aristotle, God can only be described as engaging in the highest activity (thinking), and that directed to the highest object (himself). Consequent to this description, it would be unworthy of God to attend to any being lower than himself; and yet Aristotle goes beyond Plato in describing God as "pure activity." Further, his philosophy seems to require God, not only as the ultimate final cause of the universe, but also as its ultimate *efficient* cause as well. The opposed *a priori* and empirical committments within the Greek project to construct an adequate explanation of the world begin to bulge forward here in sharper relief; this opposition accounts specifically for the aforementioned gap, or essential incompleteness, within the Aristotelian philosophy. This, then, was the tradition, the patrimony of Greek philosophy, which Jewish and Christian thinkers inherited. Challenges aplenty it presented, but one challenge it did not present was that of assimilating a free-standing, autonomous, and *completed* system of philosophy.

Before we begin, we must say a word about the well-known "difficulty" with the texts of Aristotle, and Jaeger's thesis. The problem we have in charting the evolution of Aristotle's thought is that the texts which have come down to us are not the dialogues which he may have written (as Cicero and Plutarch tell us he did) as is the case with Plato, but lecture notes for a set of courses which Aristotle, as a teacher, retained and revised periodically in light of his insights and conclusions in different areas. Thus, for example, it has not proven easy to date the metaphysical lectures in a clear sequence. Today we can say at least that these texts were composed at different times and seem rather to have grown together, as from various points on a compass, towards a center - a center which may have been the last thing to emerge in Aristotle's thought, and that perhaps inadequately. He brought them all forward at the same time; and the presence of (earlier?) "physical" language of form and matter next to (later?) metaphysical language of act and potency apparently indicates that Aristotle did not mean to present himself as abandoning his earlier position, even if his way of expressing himself had since evolved. We must take this into account, even if we conclude that his position had changed - *especially* if we conclude that it had changed (as I do, but not for the reasons Jaeger suggests). But then the scenario becomes a different and more complicated one than Jaeger presents. The situation now is not that Aristotle changed, and simply neglected to register this change adequately in the texts, so that two thousand years of commentary were deceived into thinking he had produced *one* system; rather, he changed, but he also took certain steps to *conceal* this change. This is puzzling, for why would he do this? What would he have to hide?

This revised interpretation of the situation opens the mystery that challenges us, for its resolution, to pursue doggedly and face squarely the incompleteness of the Aristotelian program, its failure to carry through its self-given project of a "scientific" explanation for the cosmos (a failure Aristotle himself almost certainly detected) - a mystery at least as interesting as the possible rediscovery of Aristotle's supposed lost work on comedy, which has served as the subplot for Umberto Eco's well-known historical novel, **The Name of the Rose**. The main themes of this supposed lost work are not difficult to reconstruct along lines suggested in the **Poetics**, the **Ethics**, and the **Rhetoric**. The former - the foundation of the Aristotelian system - almost certainly never existed (because it could not exist), and Aristotle himself may have been the "Professor Moriarty" who went to some pains to make sure that this absence would not be detected.

NOTES

1   See, for example, G.B. Kerford's article "Aristotle" in **The Encyclopedia of Philosophy** (Macmillan, N.Y., 1967), and G.E.L. Owen's "Logic and Metaphysics in some earlier works of Aristotle" **(Aristotle and Plato in the Mid-Fourth Century)** Goteborg, Sweden, 1960), both of which conclude that Aristotle's development was the *reverse* of what Jaeger suggests, that is, from metaphysics as the general study of being, to metaphysics as theology, or the study of the highest supersensuous substances.

2   See Ch. 1, note 2. p. 21.

INTRODUCTION

It is my thesis that Plotinus provided the key that for the first time allowed the full exploitation of the Aristotelian description of God as dynamic act, rather than static form, and opened the way for the achievement of the Aristotelian project of a complete scientific explanation - complete not (only) in the sense of taking in all objects, but rather in the specific sense of covering all the important *aspects* of objects, including, in particular, their existence.[1] Of course, Plotinus did not himself carry out this revolution. Although he opened up the possibility that God could be not only active, but "infinite" (and thus the possibility that act is deeper than and not inherently limited to form), he was still in bondage to a practical equivalent of that formalism, in the observance of the Aristotelian convention of divine perfection: God must be engaged in the highest activity, and that concerned with the highest object. Thus God cannot, while remaining perfect, be taken up with anything other than himself; as a consequence, any explanation of the *world* (as a distinct reality) becomes, in principle, impossible. The strict observance of this convention led to the well-known *aporia* of the Aristotelian philosophy, which Plotinus tried to resolve by developing his twin devices of a necessary "emanation," or of a voluntary "fall," of the world from God. These are jury-rigged and also mutually opposed strategies, however, which derive from the central problem - the convention of divine perfection - and leave it untouched; as a consequence, Plotinus' revolution, although a step in the right direction, ultimately falls short, and his solution remains unsatisfying.

What is lacking and required is some account of why God would make an object distinct from himself, an account that is in accord with the trait of divine perfection the Greeks insisted upon - as the most real thing, he needs nothing else. If he makes a world, it must be with some other motive. The production of the world by itself does not seem to be of any particular interest or obvious benefit to God. What emerges, strangely enough, is that creation only makes sense if it is joined to or embedded within a wider context of "salvation" (or as the evangelist John calls it, "friendship"); that is, that an *exitus* or production of the world from God only makes sense if it becomes the first stage to a cosmic *redditus* or return of the world to God, for only such a *redditus* can provide the

7

necessary motivation to lead God to embark upon the otherwise puzzling and ambiguous enterprise of the production of a world in the first place. The task of the medieval scholastics (Jewish, Islamic, and Christian) will be to search for some theoretical device able to reconcile the Greek notion of divine self-sufficiency with the attractiveness to God of producing a world beyond himself. The suggestion of several Christian thinkers in particular (following Dionysius the Aeropagite), is that God could be attracted to the display or manifestation of his glory to creatures equipped to appreciate (and reflect back) that greatness. This suggestion widens the convention of divine self-sufficiency and self-preoccupation sufficiently to overcome the opposition to divine productivity; more deeply, the goal of "salvation" becomes the condition finally sufficient to explain creation - indeed, the *only* such strategy that is consonant with the doctrine of divine perfection as self-sufficiency.

Neither Hellenic nor Hellenistic philosophy, however, could take this step nor tolerate such a doctrine; their objection to the notion of salvation is the same as their objection to "creation": this description of God is too anthropomorphic; theoretically speaking, God's perfection does not permit this much interest in beings other than himself. As a consequence, however, the production of the world - which seems so "natural" (and thus essential) for any "scientific" account to explain - becomes a surd, an irrational, inexplicable bulge in the cosmic pattern - either a necessary but regrettable side effect of the divine nature, a stage in God's self-unfolding; or it is simply an illusion, in which case the lack of an explanation for it is not puzzling, for the world is not real after all and therefore no longer *needs* to be explained. The larger consequence for the history of philosophy, however, is that, in eschewing for theoretical reasons a doctrine of divine initiative towards a world (or in declining to consider a type of perfection distinct from and higher than self-sufficiency), Greek philosophy locked itself into a irremediable frustration in its program to develop a complete or adequate account of the world.

From this perspective, Christian philosophy did not develop merely to rebut pagan philosophy, nor even only to "reconcile faith with reason"; it also served, incidently but crucially, to repair an internal omission and a significant deficiency within Greek philosophy, to address the failure of Greek philosophy to live up to its own model of an adequate or scientific explanation of the world. Greek philosophy was stalled and stuck in the breach by its own convention of perfection; Christian philosophy functioned to break this impasse, and thus to allow Greek philosophy to move on to fulfill its internal intention and proper ambition of becoming a complete explanation. The Christian *kerygma* or proclamation did not destroy Greek philosophy (as the eighteenth-century Enlightenment maintained); rather, paradoxically, in pressing its "scandalous" thesis of salvation and divine friendship, it delivered the crucial blow that expanded and fleshed out the Greek convention of divine goodness, thereby enabling Greek philosophy to move on, finally, to its proper termination and to coincide, ironically for the first time, with its intended, natural, and properly "philosophical" conclusion.

NOTES

1   For Aristotle's understanding of "scientific knowledge," see **Posterior Analytics** 71b 10-17 and 76b 11-16.

CHAPTER ONE

ARISTOTLE AND THE ESSENTIAL FAILURE

Among recent commentators on Aristotle, Marjorie Grene has distinguished herself, not only by her thorough immersion in and mastery of the Aristotelian corpus, but also, and more especially, by her determined resolve to shed any preconceived notions and to enter as far as possible into the spirit of the Aristotelian program of explanation, to see what Aristotle's philosophy looks like "from the inside," or as she puts it, to interpret *"ARISTOTELES EX ARISTOTELE."* She describes this kind of empathetic self-displacement as the goal of an interpretation that will not distort its historical subject by missing important links between individual pronouncements, connections which only an insight into the spirit of the author can reveal:

> Critical analysis is essential to history; but it should be criticism subordinate to an aim that is essentially anti-critical: i.e., the imaginative projection of the historian into the situation of his subject, his sympathetic identification with him. While remaining ourselves, with our twentieth-century standards and beliefs, we must, if we would understand a dead philosopher, yet put ourselves intellectually in some sense in his place. (p. 30)[1]

Professor Grene's book, **A Portrait of Aristotle,** is one of the more successful recent attempts at such an empathetic understanding of Aristotle, although Prof. Grene regularly (and helpfully) calls our attention to how the modern understanding of many things, especially nature, has altered since Aristotle's day; and she herself finally reports her own inability to accept the Aristotelian outlook, although she can admire its design and interior harmony (p. 242 ff). However, she appears to jump back from the Aristotelian to the modern Enlightenment or sceptical attitude at a key juncture in the exposition. In my opinion, this displacement hinders her ability to appreciate fully the problem Aristotle is facing at that point, which I believe to be the discovery that his program to explain the world of nature is *a priori* impossible - that it cannot, in principle, be carried out. Before we take up this point in some detail, however, let us review the general development of Aristotle's program to explain the natural world, following Professor Grene as our guide.

Professor Grene begins her exposition by agreeing with D'arcy Thompson that "Aristotle's *biology* may have provided the cornerstone for his metaphysics and his logic - for *all* his philosophy, in fact - which was elaborated in teaching form years after the sojourn in Assos and Lesbos." (p. 32, emphasis mine) As Prof. Grene sees it, Aristotle begins with sensible, moving substances, conceived on the model of organic beings; further, the model of an adequate or successful explanation in *biology* provides him with his model for a successful explanation in other areas as well. Aristotle's method proceeds "outward," from the explanation of change within a single substance, to the appearance of new specimens within the same species, and lastly to the study of certain limit or "pure" substances, which he finds it necessary to posit to round off his paradigm of an adequate or successful explanation of these earlier substances, which taken together make up "nature." In other words, to attain a satisfying account of the world he can see, he finds he must posit the existence of things he *cannot* see. Summing up this hypothesis, Professor Grene presents us with her program to

> consider Aristotle the methodologist reflecting on the procedure of Aristotle the biologist, Aristotle the physicist of qualitative change, of growth, and of birth and death, generalizing from biology to "nature" as such, Aristotle the metaphysician of life, working carefully through the difficult dialectical progression from what are plainly, visibly, substances - plants, and animals, and the celestial spheres - to separate substance and the necessarily unchanged principle of all change. (p. 58)

The ultimate limits of his explanation of the realm of nature, begun in the **Physics**, are studied in the series of strangely disconnected chapters of the **Metaphysics**. The **Metaphysics** should bring the program of explanation begun in the **Physics** to an end and successful completion. Certain questions or lines of investigation opened up in the **Physics** apparently require the treatment they receive in the Metaphysics, and this treatment is supposed to round off the explanation as a whole, bringing it to completion and a conclusion. It is my thesis, however, that Aristotle discovered that he could *never* complete his program of explanation, and that he did his best, in both the **Physics** and the **Metaphysics,** to conceal this inability, to distract readers from discovering this for themselves, by changing the question bequeathed from his biological starting point from one he could not answer to one he could, so as to give the impression that he *had* satisfied the model of a successful explanation and lived up to his own canons of adequacy - and hope that no one would notice that this shift had taken place.

Aristotle announces in the texts of the **Metaphysics** that he will give us a *demonstrative* science of "being *qua* being" (1003a), which for him means both a science of all things under the aspect of their *being*, and also a study of the "highest instances of being," or the "most divine things," which he evidently considers to be the causes of being in other, derivative entities - and thus required as part of a satisfying or adequate explanation of these derivative entities. We should remember, in Aristotle's theory of causation devolving from his biological investigations, an "explanation" of something should mention *all* the things needed to actually *produce* the thing in question (198a 24; 984b 9).

Professor Grene correctly points out that, in the texts of the **Metaphysics** which we have, we never get this demonstrative science, but only a *dialectical* science, that is, one which reasons *up* to a first instance of being, but not back *down* again towards lesser, derivative types of being. Professor Grene rightly sees this as a flaw in Aristotle's execution of his project, but she does not probe further to inquire what might be the reason for this disappointing and rather surprising discrepancy between announced program and actual production. If this fact can be shown to be not adventitious or accidental, not simply the *omission* of a demonstration that *could* in principle have been provided, but rather one that is essential, inevitable, and even definitive, given the assumptions of Hellenic and especially Aristotelian philosophy, as I believe it can be, then an exploration of this unexpected turn of events will advance our appreciation of the strengths but also of the weaknesses, the possibilities but also the limitations, of what Aristotelian philosophy can be expected to explain, as well as adjusting our perception as to the correct relationship obtaining between Aristotelian philosophy and the uses and extensions made of it by later thinkers - Jewish, Islamic, and Christian - working within this tradition but also that of a revelation. But first let us examine this discrepancy between what Aristotle promises and what he actually produces, as Prof. Grene describes it:

If Wisdom is a science, its method must be not merely dialectical but demonstrative. Yet the whole of the **Metaphysics** as we have it consists of the dialectical and inductive part of first philosophy: the path to its first principle, that is, to the primary instance. For even though Aristotle arrives in Lambda at a treatment of pure separate form, that is, of the unmoved movers, he does not go further to treat the unmoved source of motion in relation to other beings, and show how it is and functions as the primary instance of being. He does not move from dialectic to demonstration and give us first philosophy itself, but only, through the devious route of a series of school exercises, the introduction to it, the road *to* first principles, which is not itself the science we seek. . . The chapter in Kappa, and other passages as well, strongly suggest that Aristotle thought of this science as not merely dialectical, as our text is, but demonstrative. Where are those demonstrations? Owens seems to think he had them but did not write them down, or that they have not come down to us. But is it not also possible that they do not exist because they could not? Because the science of being *qua* being is non-existent and unattainable? (pp. 192-3) Aristotle never makes explicit *how* pure actuality or separate substance serves as primary instance of being. Even Lambda is still dialectical: the last stage on the road to the first principles of Wisdom, not the science itself. (p. 226)[2]

Prof. Grene does not go on to specify *why* the science of being *qua* being is non-existent or unattainable; she merely raises this as a possibility we should consider seriously. Yet this suggestion can be made from various points of view; and from the brevity of Prof. Grene's observations, it is not clear from which background she is speaking. This suggestion can be made, for instance, from *outside* the Aristotelian world view, from the modern Enlightenment perspective, reflecting the Kantian and positivist position that "being" is not a meaningful predicate at all, and thus that any purported science of "being *qua* being" is and must remain an empty science, or nonsense. Alternatively, the statement can be made from *within* the Aristotelian world view, on the basis of a deep and empathetic appreciation of the structure of Aristotle's philosophy, reflecting the discovery of the incompatibility of such a science with other, equally structural or fundamental commitments within the Aristotelian program. Prof. Grene does not indicate which viewpoint she is speaking from. The contrast between the significance of her suggestion, however, and the seeming indifference or nonchalance with which it is presented, marks this statement off from the cautious and careful exposition which surrounds it, and invests it with a certain provocative character, or shock value. The discrepancy between content and style, and the resulting tart sense of understatement, suggest that Prof. Grene's intention may have been simply to startle her readers, to bring them up short, and (in the absence of indications to the contrary) without warning to confront them with the modern Enlightenment sensibility. At the very least, the statement is ambiguous, and this ambiguity may have been deliberate, perhaps as an element of style or rhetorical flourish.

Whatever her intention, I wish to agree with Prof. Grene that the demonstrative science of being *qua* being is indeed impossible for Aristotle, but I wish to do so from *within* the Aristotelian viewpoint. In other words, I wish to argue that a demonstrative science of being *qua* being is impossible for Aristotle for reasons *internal* to his philosophy, reasons of which Aristotle was probably aware but chose to ignore, cover over, or at least not publically acknowledge - probably because, on the one hand, they were an embarrassment to him (and apparently insoluble), and on the other hand because he was primarily interested in his empirical and taxonomic research, and in metaphysics only to the extent that it was necessary to round out and complete the model he had given of an acceptable explanation of the empirical world. In other words, he was "locked in," by his own logical criteria of adequate explanation, to metaphysics, even if he found that, in practice, it could not be carried out. This did not cause him undue dismay, because he was probably not excessively interested in it in the first place. Nevertheless, he went through the motions of constructing an adequate explanation, papering over his inability to deliver an ultimate efficient cause for the universe by trying to distract his readers with another piece of data, the supposed *eternity* of the world. If that device does not work - well then, too bad. His attitude seems to have been something like this: "The world is obviously real, and it has, then, to have been produced by something - even if I myself am not fully able to explain how this could be." His interest lay elsewhere - in empirical research - and he was not going to waste valuable time sorting out the difficulties involved in this purely speculative line of investigation. Like Edmund Burke mulling over the hidden virtues of the long established, slowly elaborated monarchical political system, Aristotle may have reflected: "Even if I cannot explain how it came into being, it certainly works well now and keeps rolling along splendidly." And it was in the "rolling along" that Aristotle was principally interested. Perhaps he considered his theory only a first sketch, to be extended and amplified by later thinkers working within the tradition he was opening up. As it stands, the **Metaphysics** certainly seems an unclearly organized and possibly unfinished work. Thus I wish to argue that the *lacuna* in the Aristotelian philosophy, the discrepancy between what he promises and what he actually gives us, represents something more than a simple omission, a lapse of attention, or a want of industry on his part; it is rather what Aristotle would call an *aporia* or knot (**MET** 995a 30), an apparent paradox at which we arrive by dialectical reasoning, in which antithetical and irreconcilable requirements are demanded of the selfsame reality. I believe this represents a central paradox or contradiction within his philosophy which Aristotle may have discovered, and which throws the whole set of conventions upon which his philosophy rests (and the Greek tradition which he brings forward) into crisis, and as a consequence the *project* to philosophy at that date, that is, the project to fashion an adequate explanation of the physical world, into serious jeopardy. Only an expansion of these conventions (beyond what the Greeks would consider acceptable) would later allow this project to escape from this difficulty, so that, at "un-Greek" hands, this Greek project could be taken up again and proceed finally to a proper termination.

Aristotle establishes simultaneously two very strong points: first, that God must exist as a necessary first cause to explain the world, and secondly that God, if he exists, could not cause a world significantly distinct from himself. Both conclusions are demonstrated as necessarily true, and the one contradicts the other. His results are thus not simply a *failure* to demonstrate, or to carry through a preassigned program of explanation; they rather constitute a rigorous and powerful "disproof," that is, a demonstration that a demonstrative science, or adequate explanation of the world, is *impossible,* it cannot be delivered. This is no mere temporary setback, a failure to execute a program which later thinkers, through greater industry or more diligent application, could repair. This result is definitive and final; no change can be expected in the future. Our situation is significantly altered by these results, and becomes fundamentally paradoxical: our world *requires* a first cause, and yet, a first cause being given, the project to explain the world from this first cause is seen to be *a priori* impossible. In this sense Aristotle's philosophy can be said to constitute a "deconstruction" of explanation: that is, it *appears* as though Aristotle's results are to be interpreted as the completion and conclusion of an ongoing Greek program to explain the world; but what they *really* establish, on the contrary, is that this program must be given up as a bad job, because we have now discovered that, in principle, this project cannot be carried out.

On the one hand, there is no question but that Aristotle reasons dialectically to the existence of an "un-caused cause" (which he also describes as the "first" or "highest" separate substance). His four-fold model of explanation (presented most fully in **Physics**, Bk. 2, ch. 3) requires that he reason both to a first efficient cause and to an ultimate final cause, the alpha and the omega of the universe, for his explanation to be complete or "filled out" in all directions. In the line of efficient causality Aristotle reasons (in two places3) to the existence of an "unmoved mover" (which ultimately depends upon a "pure act," under pain of infinite regress) as the necessary first cause of the universe. But statements he makes elsewhere contradict, take back, or strike down this part of his conclusions. Aristotle discovers that it is in the nature of the "unmoved mover" (as a "pure act") to be a self-contained and self-contemplating substance (**MET** Bk. 12, ch. 9). These traits evidently render it impossible for this first instance of being *ever* to venture beyond itself; as a consequence, it could never function as an efficient cause of anything. The world could be a necessary side effect of God's self-contemplation; or it could be an illusion (in its appearing distinct from God, or non-divine). However, in neither case is it truly distinct from God, or something God has done that is distinct from his nature. So the first line of reasoning, although apparently necessary and valid, is here contradicted, cancelled, and corrected by a *second* line of reasoning Aristotle subsequently develops, that is also necessary and valid. Or, more precisely, it remains true that we do need some such first efficient cause to explain the world adequately. But the need apparently does not generate the *fact*. And in point of detail, when we come to examine the nature of this first substance or uncaused cause, we discover that, for internal reasons, it could not possibly produce anything beyond itself. As Edward Zeller expressed this result a hundred years ago: "Aristotle's system . . . gives him no justification for his frequent treatment of nature (that is, a cause of its own motion) as a real power operating in the world."4 Alternatively, if the first efficient causes are *not* derived from the ultimate final cause, then we have a gnostic metaphysical scenario in which there are *two* gods (uncaused and unconditioned beings), one an "efficient cause" or "creator god" who brings the world into existence, and the other an aloof but perfect "Father God," who saves us (allows us to reverse the mistake that is creation, or "forms-in-matter") by letting us contemplate his perfect activity, and thus (since like knows like) pulling ourselves out of matter as far as we are able and up to his level. But if Aristotle's "Unmoved Mover" is really the highest "separate substance," then the "creator god" must be somehow related and even subordinate to it. The latter cannot be truly independent or uncaused; and this relationship has as a result pushing ultimate responsibility for the production of the world back to the first or highest substance. In other words, he must be the ultimate efficient cause, as well as the ultimate final cause.

A synoptic and sober appraisal of the results of Aristotle's performance would have to conclude, therefore, that the *only* part of his dialectical conclusion that is left standing at the end is God's existence as *final* cause of the universe - *not* as the efficient cause. This is the only kind of causality pure act can exercise, compatible with its nature as self-sufficient and self- contemplating substance - inspiring motion and desire in other beings, itself unmoved and desiring nothing beyond itself. It is impossible in *principle* for such a being to move *outside* itself or to cause anything truly distinct from itself (such an account becomes philosophically unacceptable for two reasons: an unintended but supposedly real spin-off of the world from God would constitute a return to mythological explanation, from which Greek philosophy is trying to separate itself; and from the other, theoretical direction, a necessary effect of God's own activity would be part of his own nature).[5] As a consequence of this "self-cancellation" or "deconstruction" of his own dialectical results, Aristotle's explanation of the world becomes formally incomplete, the possibility of an adequate account of the cosmos as an (even relatively) independent reality is taken away, and the origin of the world drops out of sight behind a veil of mystery.

Thus, this attempt to produce an explanation of the world has not only not succeeded, it has rendered our predicament considerably worse, and our situation more uncomfortable than it was before. Not only have we failed to generate an adequate explanation of the world; but we have discovered, to our great dismay, that such an explanation is *impossible,* that our situation is inherently contradictory and irrational. Our former belief in the intelligibility of our situation is here exposed as an illusion or an uncritically accepted assumption. If we may speak loosely in the modern sense of a "natural salvation" associated with *understanding* one's situation, no matter how bad it may be - even this modest "surcease of sorrow" is now denied us or has been removed as one of our options. By way of contrast, Spinoza will later write: "He who truly loves God would never demand that God love him in return"[6]; that is, even if we learn that God is an impersonal deity who could not possibly take an interest in us, that realization, that understanding, says Spinoza, should itself quiet our desire for any higher fate, any deeper form of communion or happiness; that insight should supply its own type of balm and consolation. Thus knowledge itself would constitute a kind of natural "salvation," in the sense of weakening and anesthetizing the pain it cannot entirely remove, making possible on our part an altered, yet tolerable, accomodation to existence. In a similar but more intense vein the Existentialist thinker Albert Camus expresses this same view in his well-known passage on the fate of Sisyphus: "Sisyphus . . . knows the whole extent of his wretched condition. . . The lucidity that was to constitute his torture at the same time crowns his victory. There is no fate that cannot be surmounted by scorn."[7] For Camus the universe is no longer simply indifferent, as it was with Spinoza, but now positively hostile or malicious; but still the bold insight into our condition, the unflinching recognition of our plight precisely in its most hopeless aspects, *itself* constitutes a point of triumph, a basis for dignity and pride; this knowledge provides a demonstration of our greatness, and is thus a kind of buffer or psychological "pillow," offering a sustaining energy or *élan* that permits us to meet and surmount the pain inherent in this vision. What was meant to crown our torture may in fact mark our victory over this fate, precisely by demonstrating our dignity and worth in being able to turn to face the worst in our situation; this becomes an exhibition of strength and courage that can never later be denied or taken away from us. For the moderns, man may perish, but he must go out with "head bloody but unbowed." Clear insight, unflinching knowledge, brings its own kind of pleasure or "salvation"; it achieves a paradoxical release, demonstrates its own value and transcendence, precisely by its capacity to turn and *accept* the abysmal situation in which it finds itself, and the impossibility of changing it.

But, on our reading of Aristotle's dialectical results, apparently even this modest modern "salvation" is to be taken away from us. For, if we follow Virgil's lines in the **Georgics** *"FELIX QUI POTUIT RERUM COGNOSCERE CAUSAS"* (or "Happy the man who knows the causes of things"), then our condition must be candidly confessed to be definitively *un*happy, for we have now learned that knowledge is denied us, we have discovered that we cannot know the causes of things, that there *is* no efficient cause to the world, although the world apparently needs one. If we had never *tried* to explain the world, we would have been better off, for we would at least have been spared this devastating insight, this tragic revelation of our metaphysical impoverishment, the paradoxical and incoherent character of our situation, from which no knowledge can rescue us (because there is *nothing* to be known); we might at least have preserved our delusion, our belief in the intelligibility of our world, our *presumption* that the world *could* be explained - a presumption which has now been stripped so cruelly from us. The attempt to explain our situation has exacerbated this very same situation, has made it worse than it was before, worse even than if we had simply failed to come up with an explanation; for we have now "succeeded" all too well, succeeded in proving something we did not wish to prove - that such an explanation is impossible, that such an explanation cannot, in the nature of the case, ever be produced. The closest analogue in modern thought would perhaps be the discovery of Goedel's theorem in mathematical logic, which demonstrated the *impossibility* of completing a program to deduce the basic sentences of arithmetic from formal logic (the plan to "ground" the questionable statements of mathematics in the supposedly unshakable foundation of truth-functional tautologies).[8] As above, this result constitutes not merely a temporary setback, but a surprising refutation of the very possibility of an entire enterprise, the definitive demonstration that what had seemed an unproblematic, straightforward project surprisingly cannot be carried out.

To recapitulate, Aristotle can establish speculatively the existence of a first instance of being, a primary "separate substance," but once there, he leaves us stranded. He cannot get us back again. To use Platonic imagery, he can reason *up* the divided line dialectically to a "One" that is "beyond Being," but once there he cannot reason demonstratively back *down* again. The reason for this is that the qualities with which Aristotle feels he must invest his highest substance make it impossible for this substance to produce anything significantly different from itself. It would be a declination from its perfection to do so. Had the perfection with which Aristotle characterizes this highest being been either higher or lower than the type he chooses, the possibility might have been left open for explaining how God produces a world. As it is, the type he chooses (perfect substance - independent, self-contained, and self-contemplative) makes it impossible for God to produce *anything* beyond himself - and hence there can be no demonstrative science of the world (or science of being *qua* being), because there can, in principle, be no connection between God and anything else. Strictly speaking, there *is* nothing else; the world as it appears to us is impossible. Either the world is a part of God, a stage in his necessary self-unfolding (which means that it is not truly distinct from God; and also how would this account differ from a mythological explanation?), or it is an illusion - and hence does not *need* an explanation. These are the only two options.

NOTES

1 Marjorie Grene, **A Portrait of Aristotle**, Univ. of Chicago Pr., 1963.

2 Joseph Owens, in his monumental study comes to the same conclusion, but suggests a reason *why* this demonstrative science of being *qua* being, which Aristotle announces, is in principle impossible for him to carry out:

What has appeared anomalous to some and amusing to others is the conclusion that in this interpretation the **Metaphysics** can lack an account of the derivation of Being from separate Entities to all other things. There is no indication that any treatises ever were composed by Aristotle to complete the program envisaged in the main series of his metaphysical writings. Such treatises would have to explain how Being is derived from the separate Entities by way of final causality to all other Entities. That as a point of fact separate Entity exists, that it imparts motion through being loved and desired, that it has no other object of knowledge than itself, that the visible heavens and the sublunar world depend upon it, that it is a plurality, that from it Being is derived to all other things, are statements made by Aristotle with all required definiteness. But how is the link between separate Entities and sensible things to be established? Certainly the starting point for the reasoning cannot be the separate Entities themselves. The definite character of their pure actuality restricts their knowledge and their enjoyment, and so their activity, to themselves alone. Efficient causality on their part is accordingly out of the question as an available link. Nor is there any possibility of deducing other things from them. They are too completely self-contained... His metaphysics had to remain incomplete. Its incompleteness was essential to it, and was not due to any accident of time.

Joseph Owens, **The Doctrine of Being in the Aristotelian Metaphysics**, Pontifical Institute of Medieval Studies, Toronto, 1957, Foreword to the Second Edition, pp. xxii-xxiii.

3   Aristotle, **Physics**, Bk. 7, ch. 1; and **MET** Bk. 12, ch. 6. It is true that in the **Metaphysics** (and in the **Physics**, Bk. 8, ch. 6), Aristotle justifies his description of the "unmoved mover" as "pure act" precisely by his doctrine of the eternity of motion, rather than by the need for this (otherwise) "infinite regress" to come to an end. But by this point the doctrine of "unmoved mover," which began as a first efficient cause, is in the process of swinging around and becoming equivalent, by the "identity of indiscernibles," to an ultimate final cause, which of course is fully compatible with, and adequately explains, the eternity of motion (once the existence of things is given). Aristotle clearly shifts the question from existence (or ultimate efficient cause) to the eternity of motion in **Physics**, Bk. 8, ch. 1 & 6.

4   Edward Zeller, **Outlines of the History of Greek Philosophy**, Dover, N.Y., 1980, p. 178.

5   Two criticisms can be registered to the suggestion that there is nothing self-contradictory about God producing an object distinct from himself merely by his own adequate self-knowledge; and these come from within the Aristotelian (or Greek Enlightenment) point of view (see **MET** 1074b 1-15). First, such a motif seems too obviously a regression to a "mythic" level of explanation, where the world is explained simply as a spin-off (e.g., made from a dead body) of a divine conflict. There is no accountability or "control" over this type of explanation, and Greek philosophy, in trying to "purify" the myths, is pointedly trying to get away from this unacceptably loose style of explanation. Secondly, if God produces an object distinct from himself unconsciously or without intending to, this seems to raise criticisms concerning his divinity from another angle, specifically his intelligence. Do things happen without his plan or intention (even if he may discover them after the fact)? Although there is nothing abstractly impossible about a god who is unintelligent, this does not

correspond to the Greek notion of divinity, or to the direction in which Greek "philosophy" was moving. The Greek Enlightenment will never so "purify" the myths about the gods as to take away intelligence. It was left to modern (Hegelian) philosophy to suggest that intelligence is something that god grows *into*.

From another, logical direction, if one thing necessarily determines another, and vice versa, then with what right do we call them two things rather than one? What is the "principle of individuation" whereby we can mark off one part of a single necessary structure and call it a "thing"? How far may we go with this process? Once (at least relative) independence is removed, the grounds for calling one "thing" distinct from another begin to appear arbitrary.

6   B. Spinoza, **Ethics**, Pt. V, Prop. 19.

7   A. Camus, **The Myth of Sisyphus**, Knopf, N.Y. 1958, p. 121.

8   See M. Kline, **Mathematics, the Loss of Certainty,** Oxford U. Pr., N.Y., 1980. See also E. Nagel & J. Newman, **Godel's Proof,** New York U. Pr., N.Y., 1960.

CHAPTER TWO

THE GREEK CONVENTION OF PERFECTION

Aristotle's failure is no isolated example or curious exception in the pattern of Greek philosophy. On the contrary, his conclusions join those of a long and distinguished line of thinkers, from Plato a generation before him to Plotinus almost five hundred years later, each of whom, in the interests of constructing and completing an explanation of the cosmos, tried to carry out a *revolution against* the inherited canons of true reality or perfection, and each of whom, in one way or another, failed. It is because Aristotle goes to the trouble of specifying in his logical works his criteria for an adequate or scientific explanation, that we are more aware in his case of the discrepancy between what he promises and what he actually delivers than we are with the others. But each of them attempts the same revolution, and suffers the same defeat, to a more or less obvious degree.

Perhaps the failure was inherent, or "programmed in," from the outset; that is, it may have been inevitable, given the way the Greeks conceived the project of explanation, which after Socrates came to be called "philosophy." This recurring limitation was thus not due to a simple error, but to an insight concerning a first, essential truth - that in some way "being" must be unchangeable, an insight that Parmenides expresses with the force of a revelation - an insight which established a primary context in which all subsequent thought was forced to take place. It was, however, an insight which masked a deeper and in some ways opposing exigency - the need to explain the origin or production of the world from this first, apparently unchangeable source - a need which could be *felt* as a need only after the systems generated from this first insight had been developed and lived through, and the inadequacy of the resulting accounts empirically appreciated. Still, even Plotinus, who was well aware of the gap that has to be crossed to construct an adequate explanation of the world, felt strong resistance and difficulty in challenging this Parmenidean convention. It is indeed the central pole that holds up the rich tapestry that is Greek philosophy; pull this support away, and the entire development of thought becomes incomprehensible. Greek philosophy consists largely in a series of footnotes to this Parmenidean insight treated as a central principle; when this falls to the ground or is seriously modified, Greek philosophy is transformed. Even in the Christian era, this convention was effectively challenged only in its narrow (Parmenidean) expression.[1] In its Aristotelian version (God's activity is restricted to knowing himself), it was never effectively overthrown; eventually ways had to be found to work around it and to come to terms with it.

Parmenides' insight left an impact upon Greek philosophy from which it never fully recovered; his insight lifted Greek philosophy above what it had been before, to a plateau from which, however, it was prevented from rising still farther - to the heights necessary, it turns out, to realize its ambition of constructing an adequate explanation of the world. Later Greek philosophers tried repeatedly to rebel against this convention, but always unsuccessfully, because they felt themselves unwilling or unable to challenge directly Parmenides' central thesis. Ultimate reality must in some sense be unchangeable. Motion for the Greeks is a sign of imperfection and derivation; it is what *has to be explained*, it could not itself be the ultimate explanatory principle, or do the explaining. How, then, could God (or the first principle) in any sense be in motion? To assert that he was would merely be to repeat and postpone the problem, to push the project one step further back, for then the task would be to seek some "more ultimate" principle that was truly unchanging and could therefore truly "explain" this first motion. They found it difficult to imagine or to adequately articulate a species of perfection higher than the brand Parmenides had described, of a type adequate to solve their problem; any type of dynamism, looked at from below, seems indiscernibly different from the "motion" he had identified as something that could not be ultimate. But this leads inexorably to an insurmountable problem. Explanation necessarily connects something derivative to something that is *un*derived. If the underived is conceived as fundamentally *changeless*, then where did the *derived* come from? How could there be anything *to* explain? The underived could not change or produce anything separate from itself. There should be nothing to explain. From this perspective, the essential (and insoluble) problem for Greek philosophy unfolds as something preordained, something "programmed in" from the outset, from the distinctive way the Greeks conceived and set up their project.

Thus, from Parmenides on, the term "Being" came to take on for the Greeks a second, technical meaning besides its common sense designation of the difference of one thing from another, or of what makes actual things different from merely possible or imaginary beings; it came also to mean the fixed, the changeless, the permanent, the reliable - whether this is accessible to sense, or only to thought. It was felt that there must be some such ultimate, underived, changeless "stuff," if the world was ever to be "explained." Change could take place within the *context* of an ultimate, changeless reality; but ultimate reality itself could only be changeless. This cultural bias toward the permanent severely restricts, indeed it narrows down intolerably, the spectrum of explanatory models available to a Greek theorist endeavoring to develop a satisfactory account of the cosmos.

The tension between an unchanging absolute element that is posited to explain things, and a changing "appearance" that is in need of an explanation, creates a gap that Greek philosophy is never able to cross successfully. From Parmenides on, the Greeks were able to reason up to a realm of "true being" or "ultimate reality," as a first condition or cause necessary to explain the world; but once there, they were unable to reason back down again, to re-connect this "true realm" to the world of appearances - which became, as a consequence, a puzzling shadow world, as unreal as it was elusive and fleeting. Parmenides has two accounts, one of "Being" or "Truth" and the other of "Seeming" or "Opinion," which he does not attempt to bring together. Parmenides' insight stunned the developing Milesian tradition, which was experimenting with various physical devices to explain how the world of appearances evolved or was generated from a primitive principle. Some posited a dynamism within the central stuff, a centrifugal whirling energy that could "separate out" in mechanical fashion the various elements we now see in the world around us; others could not bring themselves to integrate even this degree of dynamism into their basic principle, but chose to relegate it to a separate status. Parmenides' results seemed to deliver the death blow to this entire Milesian line of investigation, and indeed to pose an insoluble problem to the fundamental project to explain the world. It threatened nothing less than the death of philosophy, here at its very inception. Parmenides' disciple Zeno concluded that the realm of motion is an *illusion*, that it cannot be explained (and thus implied that the project to explanation should properly be called off).

Plato seeks to retrieve or revive this project; but to fend off the destructive relativism and scepticism of the Sophists, he is forced to invoke a realm of "Being" distinct from that of "Becoming," that is, the

"Forms," which are for him the epistemological and metaphysical bases of reality. As we tie down the wandering statues of Daedalus to their pedestals, thereby holding them fast, so we convert our shifting opinions into stable knowledge by tracing them back to their cause, that is, the "Form," which must have a corresponding solidity and permanence (**Meno** 97d). But how the Forms actually produce or cause these sense appearances remains a fundamental and finally unresolved mystery in Platonic philosophy - a problem which his pupil Aristotle soon noticed and complained about (**MET** Bk. 1, ch. 9, 991a 10-15). Sense individuals are allowed to "participate" or borrow their reality *from* the Forms; but this remains a rather vague and passive type of causality for Forms to exercise. It seems as though sense individuals take the initiative, and not the Forms, in the causative process; and our reasoning to the Forms is all done "after the fact," so to speak, and thus is of no help in predicting what appearances the Forms will "cause" in the future. This aloofness and indifference are thoroughly in keeping with the Forms' exalted status above the realm of motion (similar, in this respect, to Aristotle's "final cause"), but unsatisfying when one's paradigm of explanation requires one to explain why there are these particular sense individuals - or why there are any sense individuals at all.

At the same time, Plato cannot be depicted as merely the willing prisoner or passive victim of this Parmenidean convention. He gives signs of chafing under this restriction, indeed, of wanting to correct or rebel against it. In particular, he is aware of the gap Parmenides has opened up, and of the need for an ultimately satisfying explanation to account for the origin and the production of the world of appearances. Still, he has difficulty in implanting a dynamism in the higher realm of reality. Plato accepts Parmenides' understanding of "Being": it refers to the realm of stable reality, of permanence. In the cosmogonic myth of the **Timaeus**, Plato invokes a "craftsman" working outside and below the Forms, who looks to these and shapes a preexisting "stuff" according to their pattern. In the less mythological, or more "purified" accounts we get in other dialogues, there are occasional allusions to a principle of dynamism operating within or even above the Forms. In the **Sophist**, for example, Plato surprisingly attributes life, change, and even knowledge to the Forms themselves (249a). Plato also refers to a "One" which is "above Being," that is, above the Forms; Aristotle reports that Plato at one time tried to generate the Forms from the "One" operating with an "indefinite dyad" (**MET** Bk. 1, ch. 6). This suggests an ultimate dualism, but Aristotle's account remains lamentably sketchy. Plato also occasionally refers to the highest principle as the "Good." In the **Republic** this highest principle is described as analogous to the visible sun; it is suggested that it is responsible not only for our clear knowledge of the world around us, but also for there being a world to know at all (509b). In the allegories of the cave and the divided line, the "Good" is identified as the principle which produces and organizes the Forms (and, by implication, all else below the Forms). By calling it the "Good," Plato seems to suggest both that it is an ultimate object of desire, but also that it has a naturally productive or generative tendency, so that it may spontaneously well up and diffuse itself, or be responsible for the existence of other things. In short, Plato seems to be denying an ultimate dualism and also rebelling against Parmenides' convention; and these texts, in fits and starts, constitute a first step in that direction. However on the other hand these images and ideas are barely beyond the mythic level of explanation; they represent no more than a primitive beginning.

Plato in his own way indicates a paradigm or model of adequate explanation of the world, and then *excuses* himself from having to live up to it. Plato indicates that the seeker after knowledge who is able to ascend the "divided line" and penetrate to the fourth level of knowledge, should be able both to rise dialectically until he sees how the Forms are organized under the "Good," and then *descend* deductively, operating not by image or myth, but "by pure reason alone," following the necessary connections between the Forms, retracing his steps and returning to the world of images and appearances from which he started (**REP** 511b). As T.S. Eliot puts it in the *FOUR QUARTETS,* ultimate wisdom comes when we "arrive where we started/ And know the place for the first time." The report such an individual brings concerning the connections between the Forms would constitute a *complete explanation* of the world, precisely the account which we are in search of; but Plato, like Socrates before him, never claims to be this knower himself, but only a "philosopher," that is, one who is "seeking knowledge," not one who has already *attained* this knowledge (that title has been preempted by the Sophists). Socrates regularly informs the Sophists he is interrogating that he is himself only a novice in the ways of wisdom, though still hoping to make progress. In short, he is still on his way "up" and does not claim to have reached the top, or to know the answers to the questions he poses. This may be only a specimen of the famous Socratic irony; but it also provides him a dodge from having to produce a final account of the world himself.

By the same token, Plato can also excuse himself from producing a final or complete explanation, which he nonetheless encourages us to believe exists. In the dialogues we rarely get above the level of image or myth, or the lower levels of the divided line. Perhaps this is the full extent of the communication we can expect to take place in such "exoteric" works, that is, works intended for those outside the Academy, for an audience not yet enlightened or inclined to examine their opinions critically. The explanations that do appear in the dialogues are always put forward tentatively and cautiously, as at most "likely stories"; they are offered primarily, it seems, to make sure the investigation keeps going, to shore up our perhaps flagging spirits. They purport to give only a very general impression or sketch of what the final explanation might look like, while also irritating us just enough with a sense of their own inadequacy as to make us strain further, to attain the "true account" which lies beyond them. But they are never intended to bring the investigation to a halt. Plato was permanently affected by the decisive encounter between Socrates and the Sophists, which resulted in the former's death. This appears evident, both in the content of his philosophy and in his decision to present his inquiry in the form of dialogues. In particular, he seems to be deeply aware of the need for an ongoing moral "conversion," if the process of inquiry is to remain authentic or "on track," that is, if it is to be truly guided by the object under investigation, as this object continually makes new and unexpected demands upon us, as opposed to allowing us to call off our inquiry prematurely, as we insist on answers to our questions in the terms in which they were initially posed. Plato seems to view the desire to end the inquiry through the discovery of a final, definitive solution with suspicion, as almost a type of moral weakness or bad faith, and thus a tendency which must be actively combatted. It is indeed part of his philosophy that the final answer or object to our inquiry is elusive, and may be comparatively ineffable, that is, inexpressible in terms drawn from the realm of shadows and copies, or at least not in the way the goal of the investigation had been first formulated. It is we who must change to accomodate the object, not the object that must adapt to our crude preconceptions and mistaken first ways of approaching it - although such a discipline runs counter to our natural inclination. This emphasis infuses a contemplative, mystical streak, which indeed is a hidden agenda in the Platonic dialogues: we wish to remain unchanged by what we know, whereas it is precisely Plato's point that it is the deeper purpose and project of the inquiry to change *us*, so that we may "fit" the object. The surprising and marvelous power of an investigation properly carried out is that we may figuratively "grow wings" and ascend, so that we become worthy of our object and able to recognize it should it eventually come into view. One senses in the background of this continually maintained openness to moral conversion the presence of the Sophists as the unnamed audience and opposition to Plato's point of view. When, for example, we compare Plato's dialogues with the school lecture notes of Aristotle - who knew or cared little about the Sophists - the contrast is striking. The rhetorical concern to overcome psychological and personal resistance, the emphasis on the need for moral conversion, and the resolve to keep the inquiry authentic and progressing, grows and even displaces or eclipses the more primitive Socratic ambition to construct accurate definitions and (indirectly, or by means of them) an adequate explanation of the world.

Given the more critical or sceptical climate of the modern period in philosophy, Plato's dialogues have become favorite objects of dialectical, ironical, and deconstructionist interpretations; with Lessing and most moderns, Plato seems in practice to prefer the "eternal search" to the definitive finding. As a consequence, although he sides with Socrates in his theoretical claim that "knowledge" exists (and not just opinion), this claim seems to function in his philosophy much the way Hegel's "Absolute" functions in his own philosophy; that is, at times it seems to be merely a mirage deposited on the horizon, a lure dangling always just out of reach, that keeps us going through our (now) endless paces, but which we can never quite capture. In his **Seventh Letter**, Plato even says that he has never written down his true philosophy, because the dead letter cannot be questioned and subjected to further inquiry; and when, in his final oration, Socrates contemplates an afterlife, he can imagine no higher condition than being able to carry on there, with the participation of the heroes and poets, the same project of investigation and mutual interrogation he has found so profitable in this life. In practice, in other words, he seems to believe that no higher condition is possible for us. The divided line, then, supplies an "explanation-schema," an outline for an eventual complete explanation, a model which Plato throws out to be filled in at some later date, but which in fact he is never able to complete or to live up to himself. As it turns out, in fact, this schema remains a pledge, an "I.O.U." note, that is *never* redeemed in Greek philosophy.

Having been unsuccessful at explaining how the "One" could spontaneously produce the world, it seems as though in his later dialogues

Plato may have accepted his defeat at the hands of the Parmenidean convention, at least as concerns the highest level of reality. Behind the image of the "craftsman" or "demiurge" as the mysterious principle of activity below the Forms which Plato uses in the **Timaeus** to explain the production of the sense world, one may see the slightly less mythological "soul" as a third principle, besides the "One" and the "Forms," and invoked, especially in the **Laws** (894c), to perform this precise job.[2] Soul in previous Greek thought is a principle of self-movement or life (the two are thought of as interchangeable); all significant movement was thought to require eventually the presence of "soul" to properly explain it. Soul is used by Plato as a bridge or buffer principle between the world of motion and the higher realm of Being; its chief purpose is to protect and excuse the highest reality from contact with any entity beyond itself, and specifically with motion. Soul thus is responsible for both producing and ruling the world below it. The same objections that were mentioned against the demiurge, however, can be raised against soul. Its relations to the One and to the Forms remain unclear. Where did it come from? How was it produced, and why must it produce a world below itself, and motion? Is this production a good thing, a bad thing, or simply necessary - and thus devoid of any distinct reality and particular significance? All these questions go unasked and unanswered.

Looking at the dialogues as a whole, it is not difficult to see the pattern of a failed revolution. Plato begins by accepting the Parmenidean convention of the changelessness of "true being" or "ultimate reality." He experiments with various ways of introducing a principle of dynamism into the highest reaches of reality, but apparently finds no way to do this satisfactorily. He then seems, in essence, to capitulate, to abandon his attempted revolt. The dynamic element remains permanently displaced and external to the highest reality. In the later dialogues, "soul" - a principle outside and below the Forms - takes over more and more of the duties of explaining the production and motion of the world below. As stated earlier, Plato can reason "up," by conversion and dialectics, to the highest reaches of the divided line; but once there, he leaves us stranded. He is not able to live up to his own paradigm and reason back "down" again, by "purely rational" means, or to explain why the higher realm should ever produce anything beyond itself. For that he is forced to invoke an extraneous principle. The attempt to move from the "dualism" of the One operating on the "indefinite dyad" to the unitary explanation of the "Good" naturally diffusing itself in a non-jealous manner, fails.

The "palace revolt" Plato has fomented is put down by *internal* Greek forces; in the end Parmenides emerges, shaken perhaps, but still fundamentally in control.

In a similar way Aristotle can be appreciated as attempting to rebel against the formalistic constraints he inherits from the Parmenidean convention, through Plato; and in a sense he succeeds farther than Plato did. He substitutes "activity" for "form" as the deepest level of reality, or he interprets "activity" as a deeper and more adequate appreciation of what Plato's "Form" (or "Idea") is attempting to capture. However, he seems deliberately to leave his philosophy in a curiously unstable or unfinished condition; specifically, the way this "active" first principle produces other substances is omitted, or is alluded to indirectly and sketched in only the vaguest terms (cf. **MET** 993b 27-30). The most likely explanation is that, in his appreciation of the divine nature, the Parmenidean convention of true being reasserted itself in a surprising way, God had to be described as engaged in an act of perpetual self-contemplation; and it was difficult for Aristotle to discover any way in which such a being could produce anything outside itself. He did not want to retreat or back away from his general paradigm of an adequate explanation, however, which requires a first efficient cause for the various species of the universe, even though he realized he could not at the moment provide such a first being. Neither side of the opposition could be denied, and yet he could currently see no way to reconcile the opposed demands. He seems in the end to have compromised and simply postponed the search for a final reconciliation; he brings both results forward, attempting to disguise the need for a first efficient cause by stressing the eternity of motion, and underlining strongly the activity of the highest substance - as if this "hand-waving" type of explanation would do the job, or suffice (for the time being) as an explanation. As Zeller explains this strategy, "This theory of the eternity of the world, which was first formulated by Aristotle and pervades his whole philosophic system, makes the cosmogonic part of physics superfluous for him. He does not have to explain the origin of the world but only its composition and structure."[3]

On the most benign interpretation, Aristotle was perhaps simply waiting for more time, for one more redaction of his lectures, when he could have another "crack" at this problem and work out a more satisfying solution. On this interpretation, he might be using the word "activity" as a marker for a section in his texts he hoped to get back to and elaborate in more detail when he had both the time and the inclination. This hypothesis would account for the strange organization (or rather *dis*organization), the discrepancy between announced program and actual performance, which we find in the texts which have come to us as the **Metaphysics.** All of Aristotle's lectures display signs of multiple layerings and repeated editions; with their frequent cross-references, they seem to have been perpetually "works in progress." Perhaps he was counting on more years of revising and more occasions to ponder this problem; for the present he was content to simply bring forward the different pieces of the puzzle, without indicating either that the problem *was* definitive, *or* that he had found a solution. The general word "activity" is used both as a "flag" for the problem, but also to indicate the generally optimistic shape of a solution he hoped to develop in more detail when the opportunity presented itself. He was waiting for a future occasion when he himself, or individuals working later within his tradition, might find a breakthrough where currently the solution eluded him. Death may have interrupted his research before he could find the resolution he was looking for. Alternatively, but more probably, Aristotle attempted to use the eternity of motion to excuse himself from having to produce a first efficient cause (or he collapsed first efficient cause into final cause, rendering it only nominally distinct), because the problem was perceived to be insoluble.

An indication of this latter possibility, of the internal difficulty and the consequent retreat from his announced program (his ambition to explain the world according to the pattern of four-fold, but specifically efficient, causality), may be detected in the shift in his treatment of individual existence. Aristotle begins by rebelling against the formalistic constraints he inherits from Plato - the principle, for example, that there can be no science of *moving* objects, that a scientific account can be given only of an absolutely *necessary* object. Aristotle replaces the Platonic concept of "Form" with *"OUSIA"* (individual entity, substance) as the fundamental unit of reality. Anything that is real is either a substance or is dependent upon substance, as are the nine accidents. Aristotle relegates "form" to a second (and dependent) order of reality, elaborating thereby what he sees as a more economical explanation for the natural world (explaining the same data with fewer hypotheses). He carries forward the Platonic idea of form, but attempts to "immanentize" or contextualize it (as "secondary substance") within that of primary or *individual* substance. Sensible substances are in motion, but this motion is not as radical as previous thinkers had assumed. On the contrary, it is regular - necessary in the heavens, "usual or for the most part" here below the moon - and directed for each changeable substance towards a goal, which can also be called its "form." Thus, there can be a *science* of nature (which science is called "physics"), and in fact, after the study of logic, nature, or moving substances, should be the *first* object which the project to explanation takes up. It is prior in the order of knowing, as Aristotle would say, if not prior absolutely, or in the order of being.

In his criticism of Plato, Aristotle stresses the individual character of primary substance, or a substance's existence, as a trait which is not covered or explained by its form.[4] As he writes in the **Posterior Analytics**, "Definition exhibits one single thing (viz., the form), (but) what human nature is and the fact that man exists are not the same thing." (92b 8) Form can explain what a thing is, and perhaps where it is going; but it cannot explain why a thing is, or where it came from. Form can account for the regularity of motion, it cannot explain why there are moving substances in the first place. In the study of non-moving objects, as in mathematics, form constitutes a complete account; but among moving substances, form is only part of what we expect from a full or exhaustive explanation. In this regard, Aristotle operates with a strong sense of "cause"; that is, the complete list of "causes" of a thing must mention all the elements one needs actually to produce the object in question (198a 23) - which, after all, is what nature does - and we are investigating "nature" (*"PHYSIS"*). Thus the question of the **Physics** (What is nature?) is primarily the question into the *causes* which produce a thing. This science has to account both for the *individuality* of things, and also for the fact that their motion is so regular - that is, amenable to scientific study. As we will see, because Aristotle cannot produce a *first* efficient cause which can account for the individuality (or existence) of things, he gradually shifts the question which guides his inquiry from the first aspect of nature (individual existence) to the second (the regularity and hypothetical eternity of motion) - primarily because the second aspect not only distracts us from the need for a first efficient cause in a finally adequate explanation, it seems positively to do away with such a need and to rule out such a first cause. If motion (and hence nature) is regular and eternal, then there was no beginning, no time when it was not - and hence (it can be argued) no first mover (apart from final causality).[5] The request for such a cause should weaken and die away, as we realize that the question is out of place and illegitimate.

In his logical works, Aristotle treats "existence" as the *preeminent* datum about the sense world which needs to be explained in any adequate theory. Existence is what an individual substance possesses that any more universal item lacks. Further, the existence of individual substance seems to be the cause of such existence as any more universal or accidental items possess. In the **Categories** he writes:

> There are things which are neither present in a subject nor said of a subject, such as an individual man and an individual horse, for . . . that which is an individual and numerically one is not said of any subject. . . Everything except primary substance is either predicated of primary substances, or is present in them; and if these last did not exist, it would be impossible for anything else to exist. (ch. 2 & 5)

The *form* of a substance seems to condition or explain the form of the properties it may contain; but it is the *existence* of substance which even seems somehow to be responsible for such existence as they have. This is Aristotle's way of saying that accidents cannot exist apart from substance; but this stress brings out his sensitivity to existence as an order of dependence distinct from formal dependence.

Individuals of the same species differ from one another not in their form but in their existence; and Aristotle must be successful in cultivating a sensitivity to existence as a trait or aspect distinct from form - to the *difference* that existence makes - among his readers, if his criticism of Plato's Forms, and his theory of the primacy of individual substance, is to be telling and persuasive. Existence must come to stand out in bold relief in the reader's consciousness as an aspect of things similar to and yet unlike their other empirical properties, such as color, shape, weight, etc. Existence is special in that it is the only empirical trait for which Aristotle will tolerate a "Platonic" style of reasoning to a cause which is a distinct, transcendent substance (as opposed to an *immanent* principle); otherwise, he consistently opposes such a Platonic style of speculation as uneconomical. The explanation for this is related to Aristotle's basic point that *all* existence requires reference to *substance* to be fully explained; substance is understood here as something self-subsisting, or independent ("separate"). It can exist in degrees, but necessarily refers in the strong sense to a totally independent being. This standard reflects Aristotle's softening of Plato's requirement for an explanation: a scientific account need not be of "necessary" objects, yet still can only be given of something that is at least relatively *substantial.* There can be no explanation, or Aristotelian "science," of accidents by themselves, as in the modern, Humean sense where "cause" means only "constant conjunction." The warrant for writing a book *beyond* the **Physics** is the fact that sensible substances, which are "primary" from the point of view of their accidents, are discovered to be not *absolutely* primary, or not ultimately self-sustaining (**PHY** 259b 7-17). That is, (like accidents) they did *not* bring themselves into existence but are dependent upon some wider cause or object; this insight justifies, on pain of infinite regress, the posit of some truly ultimate or "primary" separate substance (a substance that is *truly* a substance, or *absolutely* independent), on which they depend. Until this object is reached, sensible substances have not yet been adequately "explained." Significantly, to express the dependence of sensible substance upon fully "separate" substance, Aristotle resorts to the same language he has used to express the dependence of *accidents* upon sensible substance, "Indestructible things, then, exist *in actuality.* Nor can things which exist of necessity exist potentially; and these are indeed primary, for if they did not exist, nothing would exist. (**MET** 1050b 17) Clearly, these first substances are looked upon as bestowing "Being." The **Metaphysics** will study (as far as it can be studied) the nature of this ultimate kind of reality. Thus the examination of the widest category which binds objects together, their existence (or the study of being *qua* being) must also, for Aristotle, necessarily and simultaneously be the study of the ultimate *cause* from which they derive their being. For only as commonly derived from this one being do objects share enough in common to qualify (barely) as the unified subject matter of a single Aristotelian science (which must normally mark out its subject matter by genus and species); and reciprocally, only through its *effects* in ordinary objects may this separate, transcendent cause of being be glimpsed, and its salient features described. Thus, to raise the question of existence, unlike other traits, is for Aristotle unavoidably to raise the question of *origins* - ontological origins of dependence, if not necessarily temporal or physical origins, although we will see that they are, for him, related.

We have a right and duty to reason to an "unmoved mover," a first separate substance; and then we have a right to study as far as we can the *nature* of that truly first substance, in particular, to see how it could be the cause of other, dependent or moving substances. Unfortunately, as mentioned, when we get to the **Metaphysics** or the study of first substance, Aristotle leaves it ambiguous or undefined *how* this could substance, Aristotle leaves it ambiguous or undefined *how* this could happen; further, his description of God's activity as "thought thinking itself" even seems to pose an insurmountable obstacle to this production. The only "causality" that God could exercise is through knowledge; and his knowledge must necessarily be of himself. Thus the highest separate substance, although "pure activity," is engaged in an act directed entirely upon itself, so that no part of its energy or attention escapes his own boundary. As an explanatory principle this highest substance becomes, in effect, a black hole, useless in trying to account for why there exists anything besides itself in the universe. God *absorbs* all energy, he generates none that could escape his periphery. God could operate as a *final* cause, but apparently not as an efficient cause. Ironically, but not surprisingly, Aristotle's "separate substance" is in danger of falling victim to the same criticism he has leveled against Plato's "Forms": "So there is no gain even if we posit eternal substances, like those who posit the Forms, unless there is in them a principle which can cause change." **MET** 1071b 15)

Given this dilemma, the hypothesis of the eternity of motion becomes distinctly attractive, indeed, it even seems to come to the rescue. The eternity of the world removes the problem of delivering a first efficient cause, because it appears to leave no room for one. Also, the hypothetical eternity of the world can be entirely explained by *final* causality: the eternity of motion in nature is the best approximation which finite, perishable substances can make to the unchanging "pure activity" of the first separate substance, the highest instance of being. The latter moves objects by attraction and the desire to imitate its own perfect activity, itself remaining unmoved and unperturbed, fixed in permanent self-enthrallment. Like everything else in the universe, its attention is directed upon the highest object around - itself. Thus change is entirely explained. And its "pure" activity is described as exhausted and needed to explain the *eternity* of motion, not where the world came from.

In the **Physics**, Bk. 8, ch. 1, Aristotle says that motion must be eternal, because if it were not, motion itself would have to come into being, there would have to have been a "motion (or coming into being) of motion," and this is impossible. Aristotle seems to be making two basic points. First, if we assume that the first (unmoved) mover had once existed *without* his circle of imitating (moving) substances, then what could have prompted him at one time to bring them into existence? Aristotle's point seems to be that there is no "sufficient reason" for the unmoved mover suddenly to decide to bring them into existence at one moment in his existence rather than another (or, if they are self-starting, for them to come into existence at one moment rather than another). This point is easily answered from within his own theory; for time is only the measure of motion. Where there is no motion, there is no time, so that before the production of the universe, there was no time. All discourse about the first substance must of necessity use terms in an extended sense, for example, use temporal terms for a non-temporal reality. Time and the universe must be co-extensive; further, there is nothing contradictory about the universe (and thus time) being eternal. Even Thomas Aquinas admits that the world could have existed from eternity, and still have been a *free* act. Freedom for us requires a separate temporal act, but this is not necessarily the case with God, whose chief characteristic is his utter simplicity (which is not really a positive trait, but just a way of marking off his total difference from us). Thus, the existence of the world from all eternity does not for Thomas necessarily mean that it was a *necessary* act on God's part, one that was required by his essence (although it must for Aristotle, because for him God can*not* have any interest in a world distinct from himself. If there *is* such a world, it must then have existed as "long" as God has existed, or be co-terminous with God [part of his nature], since it cannot be the result of a free act.) Eternity is not that threatening for Thomas.

Secondly, Aristotle seems to suggest that to entertain and tolerate the idea of a "motion of motion" is to let in an unacceptable infinite regress. This objection is a variation on Aristotle's "Third Man" objection to the Platonic Forms; in both cases the objection is, if we allow (and require) some underlying process to link form to sense individual (or to get a first motion going), that underlying substrate (or that first motion) *itself* becomes a "thing" which has to be produced in its own right (or a "motion" which has to be gotten started), and this process goes on to infinity. Each new postulation brings with it a new need or requirement, and we never reach a "substance" (something containing *itself* the cause of its own motion or being) that could begin the whole process. When we finally do postulate such a first substance, we realize that it could move only by *final* causality, not by efficient causality, which brings the whole problem round again. We are in the end forced to realize that the world must be co-eternal with God, an unintended but necessary part of his nature. By the exhaustion and elimination of the alternatives, this is the only possibility left.

Aristotle is "muddying the waters" here. Calling motion "real" is not equivalent to making it into a "thing," in the sense of a substance - and not necessarily into a *dependent* substance at that, something that would require *another* substance to get it going. Nor, for that matter, does making motion *eternal* suddenly and miraculously make it *in* dependent, as *not* needing something else to explain it. This is a too simplistic analysis of the problem, one unworthy of Aristotle, which he perhaps resorted to because he could not provide a source for the coming-into-being of a moving world. Aristotle is invoking his argument from infinite regress in an illegitimate way, for motion is not a "thing" which requires another "motion" to get it started if it is not eternal. Rather, this way of describing the situation obscures the more basic point that even to adequately explain the "first" motion we must postulate a "first mover" active not merely as substrate or in the sense of "final" cause, but also as "efficient" cause (or as *source* of a distinct object), for otherwise there would be no "potentiality" *distinct* from "act" to be transformed *into* act (which is what motion for Aristotle *is;* and God is pure act, so that a world capable of motion must first be produced as distinct from God). In a sense, Aristotle's criticism is a commentary on the weakness of his own theory, because, by his "doubling" of motion, Aristotle indicates that there could be nothing within the "first" motion that could get the whole process started - which on his theory is correct. In fact, there could be nothing within or without the series that could get the whole process started (The various "unmoved movers" are left to be the efficient cause of themselves; and yet a thing cannot cause itself.) Thus motion itself is impossible (and not just a "motion of motion," whose possibility is made to seem ridiculous, and whose unreality we are thus more willing to accept). The "substance" Aristotle's theory of motion requires, the "unmoved mover" that nevertheless moves by efficient as well as final causality, is the true reality hiding behind the phrase "motion of motion," which his theory is unable to provide. By making it appear ridiculous, Aristotle hopes to obscure this omission (or make it look like it is not a serious omission at all), to distract our attention, and to let himself off the hook of having to provide such a substance.

By exhaustion and default on the alternatives, we can say that what is ultimately needed is a notion of "creation" as distinct from "motion of motion." If creation were a species of motion, it would require a previous principle of matter, substrate, or potentiality. One could then ask, where did *that* principle come from? If the only category available is that of "motion" (as in Aristotle's system), then it itself requires a previous principle of matter to be fully explained, and so on to infinity. Thus (ironically), what Aristotle's attempted *reductio ad absurdam* argument really establishes is, not that motion is necessarily eternal or has no beginning, but rather that we need some other category besides "motion" to fully account for a moving world; that is, it establishes the need for a first beginning point that is not itself an instance of motion - exactly the opposite of what he believes it establishes. As Fr. Copleston discusses this contrast between "creation" and "motion":

> The objection that out of nothing comes nothing is, therefore, irrelevant, since nothing is looked on neither as efficient cause nor as material cause; in creation God is the efficient cause and there is no material cause whatsoever. Creation is thus not a movement or change in the proper sense, and since it is not a movement, there is no succession in the act of creation.[6]

Under the impact of this disturbing theological requirement, then, Aristotle may have realized that he would have difficulty accounting for the production of the world. He would thus have to "back track" and suppress the sensitivity to existence or origins he had raised earlier, if his *inability* to provide this first efficient cause was not to become an object of scandal, and the undoing of his highest or "first science." Specifically, he must reverse himself on the question of whether the "existence" of a thing can be explained exhaustively in terms of its *form*. He must now try to *suppress* the sensitivity to existence as a *distinctive* attribute of an object, which he had before exerted himself rather strenuously to arouse; he must now try to push it back *into* the object (specifically, into its form), like some jack-in-the-box that has popped out inopportunely. The difference that "existence" makes must now be ignored, covered over, or suppressed, because it raises the question of origins or efficient causality, a question to which Aristotle now sees he hss no answer; this inability must be somehow camouflaged or disguised; the question must be made to disappear.

Aristotle's method of suppressing the sensitivity to existence is not by denying the trait outright, but by subtly distracting and deflecting our attention to something *else*. Whereas ostensibly the question into efficient causality in the logical and physical works was meant to account for the *existence* of a particular sensible substance (in contrast to its form), slowly the *datum* that the efficient cause is supposed to account for changes, to become the *motion* of sensible substances. "Motion" in

Aristotle is used in a variety of senses. In some instances it is a synonym for the generation and destruction of an *individual* substance, which Aristotle identifies in the logical and physical works as what has to be accounted for in any adequate explanation of nature (whether the process of reproduction be eternal or not). This requires the specification of four-fold causality (and eventually of a first efficient cause) if the explanation is to be complete; in this sense, "motion" becomes a synonym for "existence," and the inquiry to explain the production of individual substance (the inquiry into "nature") may be adequately expressed as the inquiry into its "motion."

However, the term "motion" can also be used to shift our attention to *another* aspect of the coming-to-be and passing-away of individual substances, one that is not highlighted or raised to the forefront of consciousness when we are trying to account for *individual* substance. Aristotle states that the process of coming-to-be and passing-away is *eternal*. Whether he is correct or not, his repeated insistence pushes this *other* aspect of the situation before our intellectual gaze, not as an explanation, but as a datum that itself stands in need of an explanation. In the substitution, however, the individual is largely lost to view, over-whelmed, submerged, and virtually sacrificed to the pattern of the eternal regularity of the species. The two traits are certainly mutually *distracting,* if not necessarily mutually exclusive; that is, if we concentrate on explaining the pattern of the species, the existence (or the importance) of the individual necessarily falls from view and is lost to consciousness. And if we concentrate on explaining the individual substance, the pattern of the species around it (eternal or not) becomes a matter of comparative indifference. Apparently we can focus on one or the other datum of the (single) situation, but not both simultaneously; if we get one clearly in focus, the other must necessarily fall out of our field of vision. As a consequence, our inquiry must take either one or the other as its lead datum in the investigation of "nature," but it cannot take both at the same time. When we switch from one to the other, we must back up and make a fresh start. It is my contention that Aristotle began his inquiry in search of an exhaustive explanation of the *individual* substance (which requires, over Plato, an account of its *existence*), but gradually let this investigation shade over into an inquiry into the *eternity* of motion, because this second inquiry allows him to conceal the fact that he cannot provide a first efficient cause for nature. The "first separate substance" he is able to deliver cannot function in this capacity. This switch is possible because both terms or aspects of the situation are covered under the general term "motion" and the cultivated ambiguity in its meaning.

What we have, then, in the Aristotelian texts is not really a "system," not even a single investigation, but rather an inquiry into the production (or *existence*) of individual substance pursued as far as it can be, until it is seen that this inquiry cannot be carried to its completion, that the explanation according to this paradigm cannot be produced or achieved; at this point the inquiry is subtly and without proper announcement shifted in the direction of an inquiry to explain the *eternity* of motion - a hypothetical and (possibly) valid aspect of the situation, but one nonetheless requiring a *distinct* investigation. Aristotle tries to conceal the transition, however, and to pass off the second as continuous with and indeed as the culmination or fulfillment of the first investigation. In reality, though, it functions to cut off, conceal, or remove the final stage of the first inquiry (or rather the fact that Aristotle is unable to execute this final stage). This switch is thus a device Aristotle uses to save himself the embarrassment of admitting a major omission in his theoretical account of the world. This particular strategem is attractive to Aristotle because the eternity of motion removes the need for a first efficient cause; on the contrary, this new datum can be explained exhaustively in terms of *final* causality alone. Thus the absence of a first efficient cause has less chance of being noticed and missed. The term "first cause," or its equivalents ("first mover") are retained by Aristotle, but gradually become indiscernible in their effect from an ultimate *final* cause. The umbrella term under which the switch is made, the general notion used equivocally to refer both to existence and to the hypothetically eternal rotation, is "motion."[7]

Until this time Greek philosophy had been open-minded or undecided on the question of the eternity of the world, while nevertheless pursuing an investigation into the *origin* of the universe, that is, how the universe as we see it has developed, evolved, or separated out from some original "stuff." Aristotle appears, however, to want to enlist and use the eternity of the universe to cover over his strategic failure to produce a first cause of being, or to satisfy his paradigm of an adequate explanation. That is, his repeated insistence on the fixity and eternity of species is not simply a ploy to ground knowledge against the sophistic charge that the motion in the world is a radical flux; in addition to that, Aristotle can argue that, if the processes of nature are indeed eternal, then there was no beginning to the motion of the universe, so that no first efficient cause has to be provided. Under the force of this insight, the *request* for such a first efficient cause should be seen to be illegitimate, and the question itself should slowly evaporate or wither away. Reasoning the other way around, if it is found that the first cause we reason to dialectically *cannot* produce a world of nature - well, there is no harm done, for it is now seen that it does not *have* to produce a world - because nature is eternal, it *had* no beginning. The consequences of Aristotle's failure are softened or minimized, as the awareness of a *need* for a first efficient cause is denied, or at least psychologically minimized. In sum, if the processes of nature are declared to be eternal, then there is no need for (nor even any *room* for) a first efficient cause - and as a consequence no one will perhaps notice that none has been provided.

Aristotle is obviously collapsing two senses of "beginning" here, the one referring to temporal beginning, and the other to the sense of ontological dependence or derivativeness, whether this ontological causality is exercised in time or not. At times Aristotle gives signs of recognizing the difference between these two senses of "beginning," although at other times he seems to want to run the two together. It is possible for a thing to be temporally eternal and yet to be ontologically derivative, although Aristotle tries to identify the two and to interpret the former (the lack of first temporal cause) as removing the need for the latter (a first ontological cause). It would be fair to say that the two senses of "beginning" had not yet been adequately clarified and differentiated, had not as yet clearly separated themselves out in consciousness; yet it also seems to be the case that Aristotle is trying to play upon this confusion and to use the former (an hypothesis) as if it were a fact to deny the need for the second - and to excuse himself thereby from having to deliver his promised first efficient cause for the universe. By way of contrast, Thomas Aquinas will declare that even if the world is eternal - that is, if it has no temporal beginning - it would still have to have an ontological origin, which must be investigated if we are to deliver a complete explanation of all the salient features of nature. God could have chosen to create the world either way, he held, with a temporal beginning, or existing from eternity. Thomas felt that scripture decides the issue; God chose to create the world so that it has a temporal beginning as well. Most scripture scholars today would not hold that such a cosmological thesis is part of the essential meaning of **Genesis**; but Thomas' distinction between a temporal and ontological origin is still relevant to this issue.[8]

In the wake of his theological description, in the **Metaphysics** Aristotle falls back to a (perhaps deliberate) indeterminate position, and attempts to enlist the eternity of motion to make his failure to produce an efficient cause less glaring. The notion of a first separate substance, or the highest instance of being, is described as pure form *and* as pure activity (**MET**1050b 2). These are taken as equivalent expressions, although the "Platonic" description of God as "form" retracts and takes back much of the liberating promise Aristotle has packed into the term "activity" (*"ENERGIA"*). The fact that God is described as "active" seems to leave open the possibility that God could have produced a world, if he had had an adequate motive for so doing. Aristotle simply is noncommittal at this point. It is not that he denies that God did produce the world (which on his assumptions he perhaps more honestly should do), he just does not choose to express himself either way. His attitude seems to be, "Let the reader interpret these passages any way he wants to. If there are still some students who have not had their sensitivity to existence blunted or suppressed, or who retain some question about the ultimate efficient cause of the universe, well then, let them interpret this term ("activity") in any way that pleases them." It is as though Aristotle left his work deliberately under-determined or incomplete, not coming to conclusions he could and perhaps should have come to, so as not to offend our logical expectations, and also so as not to reveal the opposition and switch between the two senses of "motion" he has made within his own investigation, a switch made precisely to conceal his inability to deliver a first efficient cause for the cosmos.

As stated, the liberating energies opened up by describing God as "pure activity" are effectively diffused or compromised when Aristotle describes God as "pure form." Form is no longer subordinated or contextualized by act; rather the two seem to be on the same level or to be regarded as equivalent expressions. A choice between them is made for reasons of convenience, not because of a fundamental difference in meaning. Form is now held to explain successfully everything about the world we could want to have explained. In effect, we have regressed to a species of Platonism, in which the offensive nature of motion (and attention to the individual character of existence) has been softened or removed by making motion eternal - and thus sharing as closely as possible in the permanent and stable nature of "form." The sensitivity to the difference of individual existence, along with the interest in the origin of the universe, has been effectively lost or given up, and the question

accordingly psychologically suppressed. Aristotle here apparently takes
back the criticism of Plato he has made in the logical and physical works,
his charge that it is not clear how "form" acts as the cause of these
particular sense individuals.   At this new juncture, it is apparently
Aristotle's position that form bestows *both* intelligibility *and* existence
upon the individual[9]; there is no need for a distinct order of causality
besides form.   Form wears two hats, or does two jobs.   Indeed, the
sensitivity to existence, opened up earlier, is here successfully covered
over and capped again. There is no longer even an *awareness* that form
must now carry out two jobs, for there is no awareness of any *second* job
that form must be doing. In a parallel simplification, efficient causality
merges with and disappears behind *final* causality; though nominally
distinct, in their effects the two are now indiscernibly different. Final
cause is the only one left standing, and Aristotle effectively *identifies*
efficient cause with it, again under the deliberately ambiguous term "first
cause," or "first mover."[10]

Motion, by being made eternal, escapes the stricture of unreality it
had borne when it was understood as radical flux; but it also loses its
reference to the individual, who begins to sink back behind the general
recurring pattern; and it is the pattern upon which concentration is now
fixed and which seems to call for an explanation. Thus motion is made
no longer threatening, first by making it regular, that is, stable enough to
be the object of a scientific inquiry; secondly, by accentuating eternity as
precisely *the* datum which has to be accounted for. Attention is drawn
away from the individual to the pattern, and the pattern can be adequately
covered or explained by *form*.

There is a fundamental gap between the central gears in the Aristotelian philosophy, so that they never really make contact. There is a gap
between what God *needs* to do, and what his perfection, as Aristotle
conceives it, will *allow* him to do. Aristotle's God fails to meet the
requirements of his own philosophy, not by being imperfect, but by being
too perfect, or perfect in an inappropriate way. As long as God is perfect
in *that* way, there is no chance of his generating a universe, and hence of
there being any explanation for the production of the world. It is clear
that, at least in some passages, Aristotle wants to allow for some activity
or initiative by God; for example, towards the end of the **Nicomachean
Ethics** he writes:

A man whose activity is guided by intelligence, who cultivates his intelligence and keeps it in the best condition, seems to be most beloved by the gods. For if the gods have any concern for human affairs - and they seem to have - it is to be expected that they rejoice in what is best and most akin to them, and that is our intelligence; and it is also to be expected that they requite with good those who most love and honor intelligence, as being men who care for what is dear to the gods and who act rightly and nobly. (1179a 22-29)

Traditionally, *any* kind of dynamism was thought to stain or compromise God's perfection, to disqualify God from being "God." Aristotle has the machinery, in his distinction between "activity" and "motion," to challenge this broad prejudice and to introduce a dynamism into God without compromising his perfection; he initiates this transformation (and indicates his intention of doing precisely this) by calling God "pure activity." But he fails to follow through on this initial step, and in a sense, "un-does" the promising start he has made when he comes to describe the specific activity God is engaged upon. God returns to being an island, as aloof and purely formal as he was under Parmenides' description of Being. (Aristotle knows and brings forward another tradition; in the **Meteorology** 4, 3 (380a 12 ff) he says that a thing is perfect when it can reproduce itself. However, he could apparently find no way to bring these two descriptions of perfection together. Hence, God's activity is defined exclusively as self-thinking thought.)

To bridge this gap, to resolve this difficulty, we must get inside and "pry open" the divine perfection. We must find some way to allow God to know other things besides himself, *without* thereby slighting his perfection. But, as with Parmenides' insight, we cannot simply jettison or dismiss Aristotle's description of God as an error; we must remain faithful to the truth he has uncovered. God *is* the highest object in the cosmos, and he is properly preoccupied or taken up exclusively with himself. This insight can never be abandoned or discarded. The task now will be to find some way to allow God to know other things through knowing *himself,* and yet not to reduce these things to merely necessary effects of his nature. So far, however, this description is merely the expression of a problem, not the formula for its solution. It does, however, set the agenda for the next stage in the development of Western philosophy, it points towards a specific direction in which Greek philosophy must move in its effort to extricate itself from the apparent dead end and impossible situation in which it has now wedged itself.

The universe becomes a smooth-spinning top, eternal and regular, with the outermost substances circling a first separate substance, like the rings of Saturn - the center self-contemplating and changeless, operative only as a final cause. The eternity and regularity of the motion of lower substances, stressed by Aristotle over Plato and earlier thinkers who were biased against motion as an object of knowledge, serve effectively to distract, overshadow, and smother our sensitivity to existence, aroused in the logical works, and the question of origins or efficient cause, raised in the **Physics**. The system of nature works perfectly, shimmering in its internal proportion and harmony - as long as we do not ask where the whole thing came from. At the touch of that question, this balanced and symmetrical cosmos shatters like crystal.

Parallel to the shift in the meaning of the word "motion," the understanding of "existence" also shifts between two different meanings for Aristotle: the existence of the individual suggests *difference*, and is captured in the notion of *"act"*; the existence of the pattern or of whatever is permanent suggests substance, and is captured by the notion of "form." Attention is gradually shifted away from individual difference to a more metaphysical or Platonic notion of permanence or stability (being as *substance*, which thus can be adequately "explained" by *form*). As "motion" shifts its reference equivocally from the individual to the pattern, "being" in turn is interpreted less as *difference* or act and more as *permanence* or form. Thus ultimately, in his science of "being *qua* being," what Aristotle reasons to is a first *condition* of the world (self-subsisting substance), not its first *cause* (there can *be* no first *cause* of the universe, because the first being could not possibly produce or efficiently cause *anything* beyond itself). There is no reason given, or even possibility generated, for how the world could have come into being as distinct from God. Thus, what we get from Aristotle is, at best, only *half* an explanation. It is correct as far as it goes (formal and final causality), but it does not go far enough. It is the *torso* of the full explanation we were promised. What is disturbing, however, is that it is a torso parading as a *complete* explanation; further, it seems to suggest that nothing *further* is possible.[11] The good news is that God exists; the bad news is that he could not possibly have produced the world.

The question about being is thus neither answered nor rebutted by Aristotle; the sensitivity to being is first aroused and then subtly suppressed in the texts which have come down to us. Interest in the question simply dies away. (To that extent Jaeger's thesis is correct. However, Aristotle did not lose interest in the question; rather, he saw it was impossible to answer, so that interest in the question had to be suppressed, and its relevance denied. In practice, he shifts the notion of being from efficient to final causality. He does not begin as a Platonist; rather, and perhaps rather surprisingly, he *ends* as one.) It is a powerful commentary and indication of the success of Aristotle's clever reworking and transformation of the question that, as we read the **Metaphysics** (partly because of our puzzlement and disorientation at the sequence of topics in the chapters), nothing seems lost. A burden that was to be shared equally between efficient and final causality is now shifted entirely onto the shoulders of final causality. So gradually is this transition made (and because of the difficulty of the reading matter), that we are practically unconscious of the fact that an awareness that was achieved rather strenuously and was argued for so persuasively in the logical and physical works is now delicately covered over, and finally allowed to disappear altogether, in a strategem Aristotle resorts to under the impact of his theological insight concerning God's necessary self-knowledge, and in an effort to disguise the effects of this theological description upon his program to produce a complete or scientific account of the world.

Notes

1   This conflict between these two portraits of divine perfection came to
a head early in the Christian tradition in the discussion of the
"impassibility" of Jesus, the subject of many sermons and discourses
(and of the docetist heresy). In a sense, it can be said that the religions
which emphasized the aloofness and transcendence of the deity, and
contained a strongly iconoclastic bent as a consequence (such as
Judaism and Islam), found less to object to in the received Greek or
philosophical notion of divine perfection. For the Christians, however, with their conviction of the Incarnation, as well as the suffering
and death of the Redeemer, an easy accomodation with this description was evidently impossible. Yet they could not simply reject the
Greek notion; some more sophisticated relationship between the two
had to be worked out. One can see this being done in the following
discourse by Anastasius of Antioch (c. 570 C.E.):

Only by reflecting upon the meaning of the incarnation can we see how it is possible to say with perfect truth both that Christ suffered and that he was incapable of suffering, and why the Word of God, in himself incapable of suffering, came to suffer. .. It was necessary for Christ to suffer: his passion was absolutely unavoidable. He said so himself when he called his companions dull and slow to believe because they failed to recognize that he had to suffer and so enter into his glory. Leaving behind him the glory that had been his with the Father before the world was made, he had gone forth to save his people. This salvation, however, could be achieved only by the suffering of the author of our life, as Paul taught when he said that *the author of life himself was made perfect through suffering.* Because of us he was deprived of his glory for a little while, the glory that was his as the Father's only-begotten Son, but through the cross this glory is seen to have been restored to him in a certain way in the body that he had assumed. Explaining what water the Savior referred to when he said: *He that has faith in me shall have rivers of living water flowing from within him,* John says in his gospel that *he was speaking of the Holy Spirit which those who believed in him were to receive, for the Spirit had not yet been given because Jesus had not yet been glorified.* The glorification he meant was his death upon the cross for which the Lord prayed to the Father before undergoing his passion, asking his Father to give him the glory that he had in his presence before the world began.

Oratio 4, 1-2

P G 89, 1347-1348

Two forms of "glory" are discussed, and eventually collapsed into one. The second ends by swallowing the first. According to the first (Greek) understanding, Jesus as God is impassible. This is a valid form of glory, rightfully his. He had to "leave behind" this glory when he suffered for mankind, for in no other way could the redemption of mankind be accomplished. However, this was not simply an abandoning or descent from his divine status, for Paul is quoted to the effect that even Jesus was "made perfect" through suffering. There apparently is a form of perfection higher than impassibility. Jesus won a second and evidently higher form of "glory" at his death on the cross. But then this second "glory" is identified with the glory that Jesus had in the presence of his Father, "before the world began"! The cross. But then this second "glory" is identified with the glory that Jesus had in the presence of his Father, "before the world began"! The second portrait of God has not contradicted the first, it has merely deepened and dramatized it. That at least is the Christian claim. Only with the suffering and death of Jesus was the portrait of God rendered complete on earth. Only then could the "Spirit" (another portrait) of God be given to his disciples, who in turn are called to imitate and approximate the forth-going nature of God, to which they have been dramatically exposed.

2   This thesis is developed more fully by A.H. Armstrong, **An Introduction to Ancient Philosophy,** Methuen, London, 1947, pp. 46-49.

3   E. Zeller, **Outlines of the History of Greek Philosophy,** Dover, N.Y., 1980, p. 180.

4   See **POST ANAL** 71b 31 & 35; 76a 32-36; 87b 31; and 92b 31. See also **MET** 1029a 27.

5   When thought through, Aristotle's position on this topic becomes simply incoherent. The "unmoved movers" are the first efficient (or "moving") causes of motion in the universe, whereas the ultimate "separate substance" functions only as final cause. But then, where did the "unmoved movers" (or the "Soul of the Outermost Heaven") come from? If they are uncaused or eternal (had no coming-into-being), then presumably they are also pure actuality (actuality without potentiality); then why should they be effective as efficient causes, when the ultimate "pure act" is effective only as *final* cause (and, as Aristotle concedes, all we *really* need to explain is the *eternity* of motion, and *final* causality is adequate to account for this - unless he is secretly reactivating a sensitivity to *existence* as distinct from motion)? If they have some potentiality mixed with their actuality, then how was this potentiality produced from the pure actuality of the highest separate substance? (Where else could it come from?) Secondly, they must, as moving causes (e.g., parent-to-child) give rise to individuals of the same form as themselves; but these first efficient causes are gods, and thus far *above* all the species here on earth. Thirdly (and this one cuts deeper than the other two, or wipes out even the *possibility* of an explanation), the motion of the

cosmos is declared to be eternal, and thus *needs no* first efficient cause, *only* a final cause. Indeed, it permits or tolerates no first efficient cause. A first efficient cause is not only not needed, it is not even possible - in principle. Aristotle would have done better to revise his paradigm of explanation (four-fold causality) in view of his results; as it is, he occupies an intermediate position, where the discrepancy between expectation and performance is peculiarly obvious.

In effect, Aristotle could be said to be performing here a critique analogous to the Kantian critique of the cosmological argument, by attempting to argue that, since a substance must always have as its "efficient" cause one of its own species, and since this process purportedly goes on forever, we can never reach by this process the existence of a first "necessary" (or truly "substantial" - "uncaused") being. Thus it cannot be claimed that such a first cause is needed. Of course, in doing so Aristotle pays the serious price of violating his basic principle of the priority of form over matter, of act over potentiality, of determination over indetermination, by apparently allowing in this case an "infinite regress" in the process of explanation. Coming after Leibniz and Newton (the inventors of the "calculus," or infinitesimal reasoning), Kant evidently feels he can tolerate an "actual infinity" in his universe; but Aristotle explicitly denies this possibility in his own cosmos. Thus this strategy to escape the need for a first efficient cause involves Aristotle in a contradiction.

To recapitulate, although the claim is made in two places that we need a first efficient cause to explain the universe, the substance of this claim is gradually eroded. First, the way the effectiveness of this "first efficient cause" is concretely spelled out (or what it is useful at explaining - the eternity of motion) makes it indiscernible from the effectiveness of an ultimate final cause. Secondly, with the motion of the universe declared to be eternal, the need for, and the very possibility of a first efficient cause, is taken away. At best, by the principle of parsimony, it is a "fifth wheel," redundant and not needed to explain the smooth running of the Aristotelian cosmos; at worst, it is an illusion. There is no room for it on the Aristotelian map of the world.

6   F. Copleston, S.J., **A History of Philosophy**, Vol. 2, Pt. II (Image,

N.Y., 1962), pp. 82-83

7   In **Physics**, Bk. V, ch. 1, Aristotle uses "change" (*"METABOLE"*) in a wider sense than "motion" (*"KINESIS"*), and he says that "changes with respect to generation and destruction are not motions but changes with respect to contradiction," and that "only a change from a subject to a subject must be a motion" (in other words, not substantial creation or destruction). Similarly, in the next chapter he begins by saying that "there is no motion with regard to a substance because no thing is contrary to a substance." Here he has already begun to "cover his tracks," in that he wants to cut down his task to merely explaining what he now calls "motion," rather than "change." If successful, he thereby defines a certain problem - the coming-to-be and passing-away of individual substances - *out* of existence, or as no longer a significant datum for the adequate explanation of *"nature."* By declaring the motion of the world to be eternal, and in declaring that he only wants to explain "motion" (and not "change"), the origin of the world no longer has to be accounted for.

8   Even Plotinus makes the same point. In **Enneads** 4.8 Plotinus considers the two views that matter might be a last stage of emanation that nevertheless always existed, or that it was produced in time. Although the latter is not his own view, he seems to consider that both are possible. See J.M. Rist, **Plotinus: the Road to Reality**, Cambridge Univ. Pr., N.Y., 1967, pp. 118-9.

9   See **POST ANAL** 90a 32; 93a 4 & 17 (in contrast to 92b 10); see also **MET** Bk. VII, ch. 17. Aristotle tends to assume existence, but is still sensitive to the difference it makes. This comes out in his name for what Marjorie Grene calls his major "discovery" - the "being-what-it-is" (*"to ti nv eivai"*) of a thing, which can be grasped by understanding and made the basis of a definition (**A Portrait of Aristotle**, p. 80). Prof. Grene concedes that for Aristotle "form" and "existence" tend to coalesce (p. 250) and she further writes towards the end of her book:

        "Aristotle's God is finite through and through, wholly determinate Being, pure thought and the purest object of thought, delimited sharply from all other beings, the point of reference for our knowledge of them as beings but not, most emphatically not, the source of their existence as Father or Creator. Aristotle's God cannot love the world; he can be no more than the self-sufficient object of its love, the self-contained being which other beings imitate." pp. 246-7

Prof. Grene does not, however, mention this as a possible explanation of why there is no demonstrative science of "being *qua* being" in the Aristotelian texts.

Kant has to exercise a similar reversal on the sensitivity to existence as an important empirical trait, but for a different reason: to make room for freedom, after he has demonstrated the binding power of deterministic laws to control the motions of all objects - including humans - in the physical world. "Existence" itself is the only candidate where such a freedom can still be lodged, it is the only trait in the phenomenal world for which a determining reason cannot be given; but first the current occupant of that seat must be displaced and exiled. Thus, "existence" must be debunked as a meaningless predicate: it adds *nothing* to a concept of which it is predicated. The idea of a hundred *actual* dollars is in no way different from the idea of a hundred *possible* dollars. Now that the seat is vacated, a new occupant - freedom - may be installed in its place. In his resolution of the third antinomy (A 537, B 565), the apparent contradiction between determinism and freedom as applied to the same event, Kant is surreptitiously cultivating among his readers a sensitivity to the difference that *existence* makes, and thus to existence as a "real" or meaningful predicate; the success of his rhetoric in defense of freedom is contingent upon his readers being persuaded to overlook this reversal, or "flip-flop," on the theme of existence. Kant's reversal is in the opposite direction from Aristotle's, however: first Kant suppresses our sensitivity to existence (clearing a space for freedom), *then* he arouses it (providing a job for freedom to do, making it seem as if freedom has a real or respectable place on our "map" of reality). Aristotle first *arouses* our sensitivity to existence (his opposition to Plato's Forms as a complete account of the physical world), and then suppresses it (when he sees that his ultimate separate substance cannot account any better than the Forms for the production of the world).

10 For example, at **MET** 1049b 28-30, Aristotle is evidently using the phrase "first mover" in the sense of *efficient* cause, because he says it must always be of the same species as what is generated. But then

meaning of "prime mover" now shifted to *final* cause? If it has not, can Aristotle still claim that a "prime mover" is of the *same species* as the finite substances whose genesis he is trying to explain? Aristotle here typically leaves us in the lurch, suspended between the two interpretations.

Thomas Aquinas is more sensitive to the (perhaps deliberate) equivocation, and thus avoids collapsing efficient cause into final cause:

"In the order of actions the nonunivocal agent necessarily precedes the univocal agent. In fact, a nonunivocal agent is the universal cause of the generation of all men. A univocal agent is not the universal agent cause of the whole species, otherwise it would be the cause of itself, for it is contained within the species; instead, it is the particular cause in relation to this individual which it establishes as a participant in the species. Therefore, the universal cause of the whole species is not a univocal agent." S.T., I, 13, 5, c, reply to obj. 1.

11 I think it also appropriate to mention Augustine as a "Platonic" thinker who was nonetheless trying to arouse an adequate appreciation of "existence" as a trait not covered or explained by "form." Augustine was trained as a rhetorician, that is, as someone seeking the most effective means of persuasion for his point of view; and I believe this formation left a decisive imprint on his philosophy. Augustine is well-known for his views on original sin, the damned condition of unbaptized infants, his anti-Pelagian position, and in general for stressing our constant and radical dependence upon God, not only in the order of grace (or salvation), but also in the order of nature (our bare existence). Stressing our constant and radical *dependence* upon God may be a way of bringing out the utter *gratuity* of the divine initiative towards us, an initiative at the level of salvation, but also, and more basically, at the level of *existence* itself (or creation). Augustine perhaps can also be said to be working to elaborate a philosophy that will do justice to the datum of *existence,* and not just essence. Our existence is something we tend to take for granted and forget about. By pulling the rug out from under us, Augustine may in part be motivated by the rhetorician's ambition to find the most effective way of making us aware of a datum that *needs* to be explained, but is not being adequately handled by the received

philosophical system. In this case, the datum that is not being taken into account is *existence;* and Augustine may, by stressing our radical dependence, be trying to cultivate a sensitivity to this datum, an appreciation of the fact that existence is not self-explanatory, that we are not the source of our own existence. Faint objects stand out better against a darker background.

CHAPTER THREE

PLOTINUS AND THE RECOGNITION OF THE PROBLEM

The first step in breaking this impasse and moving towards a successful resolution occurs with Plotinus; but again, as with a rocket attempting to escape the gravitational attraction of the earth, after an encouraging early effort, the inevitable pull of the Greek convention of ultimate reality begins to reassert itself, and the impulse to escape is slowed down, arrested, eventually held fast and overcome by a retrograde pull back towards the mother planet. Plotinus' break with the Greek convention of perfection is incomplete, and as a result, his attempt at an adequate explanation of the world is unsuccessful. What we have in the **Enneads** of Plotinus, then, as we have in the dialogues of Plato and in the school texts of Aristotle, is not a complete or consistent philosophy, but the record of a failed revolution, a palace revolt in which the forces *within* Greek philosophy attempted to revamp its most fundamental assumption in such a way as to make it a more adequate and satisfying account of the physical world; but which forces in the end suffered a failure of nerve, as they found they could not bring themselves to challenge the central assumption and to make the needed fundamental change. Plotinus is able to explain the production of the world; but because he cannot seriously entertain the idea that the highest principle could have a *desire* or *interest* in having its greatness acknowledged and reflected back by an independent being equipped to appreciate it, this production becomes non-intentional and mechanical, ambiguous as to its meaning or value and even as to its reality. On the positive side Plotinus explicitly says that God's goodness requires him to love himself not only "in himself," but also "in others"; he thus indicates or sketches the solution to the opposition between the twin divine traits of egoism and altruism that will be developed by several Christian thinkers later; however, Plotinus leaves it ambiguous whether the production of other beings is a free act or not, and thus robs this potential breakthrough of its power. It remains at best suggestive. He writes:

Lovable, very love, the Supreme is also self-love in that He is lovely no otherwise than from Himself and in Himself. Self-presence can hold only in the identity of associated and associating; since, in the Supreme, associated and associating are one, seeker and sought one - the sought serving as Hypostasis and substrate of the seeker - once more God's being and his seeking are identical. **Enneads**, 6.8.15 (tr. MacKenna)

Apparently God *must* engage in a love that is both directed towards himself, but also leads him to the production of a further "hypostasis" which is both the expression and the recipient of that love. Plotinus is struggling to revolutionize the Greek convention of perfection, expanding it beyond self-subsistence to creativity and self-diffusion, in accordance with Plato's description of the Good; however, he overshoots the mark and ends by describing the world as a necessary consequence of the divine nature. He writes:

It is of the essence of things that each gives of its being to another: without this communication, the Good would not be Good, nor the Intellectual-Principle an Intellective Principle, nor would Soul itself be what it is: the law is "some life after the Primal Life, a second where there is a first; all linked in an unbroken chain, all eternal..." Things commonly described as generated have never known a beginning: all has been and will be. 2.9.3

In a sense, Plotinus succeeds in expanding the Greek convention of perfection by making God creative; but, by making this creation necessary and eternal, he in effect *collapses back* and reinstates the previous convention (and problem) of having God unchanging:

To ask why the Soul has created the Cosmos, is to ask why there is a Soul and why a creator creates. The question, also, implies a beginning in the eternal and, further, represents creation as the act of a changeful Being who turns from this to that. 2.9.8

The world is produced simply as a necessary effect of the divine nature, something God could not *help* but do, and as an inevitable stage in the divine self-unfolding. As such, it is not clear that the world is distinct from God; on the contrary, it could be said that God has simply "expanded" to absorb the world. Either we interpret the theory strictly, and the world becomes *part* of God; or we interpret the theory loosely (the world *really is* distinct from God), but then the theory seems to fall back to a mythological level of explanation. Thus, although his theory represents a recognition of the problem and a first step in the right direction, Plotinus' solution is not fully satisfying.

The first change that occurs with Plotinus is that he refuses to be confused or put off by Aristotle's obfuscatory strategy of muddying the waters. Even if the world is eternal, this state of affairs leaves totally untouched, has not yet begun to address the question of the *origin,* or the ontological source, of the world.[1] We have two choices; either the world is declared to be an independent substance (or a god) in itself, and thus we no longer *need* to explain it (it is *self-* explaining); or the world is derived from something more primitive, and then some account of it needs to be given. Plotinus, following Plato, holds that the world is certainly derivative, and he also follows Plato in trying to introduce a *dynamism* into God to account for the production of the world. But here we come to the important innovation and advance Plotinus makes in the revolution Plato has initiated, one which later religious thinkers will combine with Aristotle and exploit in such a way as to produce a solution which for the first time provides answers to the chief questions raised concerning the production of the world. Plotinus is the first thinker in the Greek tradition (after Parmenides) to declare that the ultimate "One" is better described as "infinite" rather than "finite." Although this change may not seem revolutionary to us, this description underlines Plato's elevation and isolation of the One "above Being" or the Forms, it separates God from what is merely unchanging and static; and in particular, it breaks definitively the equivalence between act and form (or finitude) by which Aristotle had defused and compromised his own revolutionary impulse. Now form and act are no longer parallel or equivalent forms of expression; on the contrary, in this perspective "activity" may be deeper and more fundamental than form.[2] (Thomas Aquinas' way of following this lead will be to say that form is *potential* to [and participates in] a distinct and deeper [infinite] principle of pure *act*).

A "second story" is thereby added to our philosophical edifice, there is a dramatic increase in our theoretical resources and sophistication. New combinations of the basic elements, and hence new explanatory models, are made available. Perhaps, for example, the world can be conceded to be eternal (explained by "form"), and a new or distinct kind of origin, or order of causality (that of *existence* as "act"), can be opened up and explored. From now on, "form" need not wear two hats or perform both functions (supplying both intelligibility and existence); another principle has appeared to divide and share these tasks. A correspondingly fuller and more comprehensive account of reality may now be attempted. "Existence" need not be collapsed back into or covered over by "form." Reciprocally, God's perfection can now be conceived in a new way, as no longer captured and exhaustively expressed by "form," but rather as allowing for an interior dynamism and complexity more adequate to the transcendence and richness of this limit reality we are attempting to describe.

There is a subtle internal connection between the doctrine of a (free) creation of the world by God (proclaimed for the first time in the Greek tradition by Philo Judaeus around the year 50 C.E.), and the heightened sensitivity to *existence* as a trait which cannot be explained or accounted for by "form," which is dawning upon thinkers during this period. After all, creation is the bestowal of (independent) existence; and adequacy to the datum of existence requires something like the notion of a free creation to account for it. (Ironically, this device constitutes, not a return to the mythic tradition, as the use of a personal category might suggest, but the only way completely to *escape* from the mythic tradition to a satisfactory conceptual explanation.) The two go together; the one implies or requires the other. "Creation" is understood here, not primarily as making something out of *nothing,* but as making something truly *distinct* from the creator, something that is not merely a logical extension or deduction from his own being, determined entirely by his essence (rather, something at least relatively independent - although this does not require bringing into existence another god). If the world is in *some* way independent of God, and not merely a necessary consequence of his nature, then its existence cannot be explained exclusively by God's *nature* (or form), it demands an independent act on God's part to explain its being. Alternatively, if God did not freely create the world, then it is not truly independent of God, and its existence can be exhaustively accounted for through God's formal properties. At this point the Greek Enlightenment resists the notion of a free creation of the world, as this seems too much a reversion to an anthropomorphic and uncontrollably fanciful or mythic explanation; but it is progressively more attentive to the *existence* of the world as a trait which stands out in bold relief from its form, and which calls for its own separate treatment in any complete analysis and finally adequate account of the world. With Plotinus the Greek Enlightenment is attempting to embrace the latter while still holding aloof from the former. The difficulty is, as said, that the one requires or logically entails the other, it draws the other in its wake as an inevitable and necessary corollary. This is the pressure the Greek Enlightenment, or movement to a non-mythological "philosophical" explanation, is laboring under and attempting to resolve.

Plotinus, like Aristotle, is trying to make room for a new and higher type of perfection for God *beyond* the Parmenidean characteristic of changelessness and self-completion. Not that these are incorrect, but they do not go far enough. This new type would be a perfection *beyond* independence or self-subsistence, a perfection that would extend to activity and the possibility of an initiative *beyond* itself. This hypothetical concept would not *contradict* the old convention, it would include all that the old description contains, but also go beyond it. The problem is that, from the point of view of the Greek tradition, this form of existence *above* changelessness can appear as only indiscernibly different from the form of existence *below* changelessness, which is also characterized by alteration or change, but with the attendant connotations of imperfection and derivation which these traits, for the Greek, have traditionally implied. Thus Plotinus goes to considerable pains to stress the difference:

> The One is perfect because it seeks for nothing; and being perfect, it overflows, and thus its superabundance produces an Other. . . Whenever anything reaches its own perfection, we see that it cannot endure to remain in itself, but generates and produces something else. . . How then should the Most Perfect Being and the First Good remain shut up in itself, as though it were jealous or impotent - itself the potency of all things.[3]

This new type of perfection is presented, not as a *lapse* or *decline* from the previous convention, but as *surpassing* it, as allowing all that was true before to still be true, and more besides. God will be said to be in action or motion, but not a motion based on *need* or *incompleteness,* as before all motion was thought to be, but just the opposite - an activity based on overfullness and generosity. (In fact, the difficulty from now on will be to keep God's production of the world from becoming a *necessary* [and hence again unfree] act of production, since it is said to be a "natural tendency" of his. Origen the Christian, a contemporary of Plotinus, argued that because God is goodness and power, he must *always* have had objects on which to exercise these attributes; hence he must have brought into existence a world of spiritual beings, or souls, co-eternal with himself. In avoiding one theoretical embarrassment [the *lack* of an account for the production of the world], the danger now is that of going too far in the*opposite* direction, and of landing, paradoxically, in the selfsame predicament: if God had to create a world, then this world is not truly *distinct* from God, it enjoys no independent existence. In other words, *again* we have no account of the production of a relatively independent world.)

All is ready now for a complete explanation of the world. So far, however, we have only *half* an explanation. For even if form is "potential" to a deeper and underlying (infinite) act, why should God choose to actuate just *these* potentialities? For that matter, why would God choose to actuate *any* potentialities at all? Plotinus succeeds in introducing a dynamism into the heart of the godhead, so that the "One" must proceed through two "hypostases" before it unfolds necessarily and fully realizes its nature; but he is unable to lead this dynamism *outside* of God in a satisfying manner, so that his God, like Aristotle's, remains ultimately closed in upon itself. The reason for this is that Plotinus accepts Aristotle's description of God's activity as that of self-contemplation, and can find no adequate way of arranging for God to know other things *beyond* himself. On his account, the world of matter is produced necessarily and unconsciously as an automatic "emanation" from God's nature. However, Plotinus does chance upon one device, which he throws out only to save God from the criticism or imperfection of not knowing something he is doing. The world consists of the necessary *effects* of which God is the non-intending cause. It would be inappropriate for God to take *direct* account of these effects, for that would mean directing his attention to objects *beneath* himself, and thus lowering himself to their level. However, it would be *equally* inappropriate for God *not* to know something that he is doing (even if without intending to), for that would mean that he is ignorant of something that is happening. Perhaps, Plotinus reasons, he can know these effects *indirectly* - "out of the corner of his eye," so to speak - and not be demeaned or "pulled down" by this knowledge, but on the contrary still retain his majestic independence and transcendent aloofness. In fact, perhaps he would *have* to do that; for, Plotinus could argue, to know *himself* adequately, God must simultaneously be aware of all the *effects* of which his nature is the necessary cause; otherwise, his knowledge of him*self* would be incomplete or partial.[4] Plotinus comments:

If the Supreme is to have intellection, it cannot know only itself; that would not be intellection, for, if it did know itself, nothing could prevent it knowing all things... It follows that the Supreme will know neither itself nor anything else but will hold an august repose. 6.7.39

Plotinus feels he must deny knowledge to the "One" for two reasons. First, knowledge threatens to introduce duality into what Plotinus insists is an absolute *unity* or simplicity. In knowledge there is always a duality between knower and object known - even in self-knowledge. Consequently, the One cannot be said to "know" even itself; this activity must be relegated to the *second* hypostasis, or *"NOUS."* But secondly, as stated, knowledge tends to make us "like" what we know; and for God to know the world would be for God to be pulled down to the world's level. This would be unworthy of God; thus even knowledge would mean too much contact with the world. But then Plotinus seems to realize that he may have introduced imperfection into God from the reverse side, or without intending to, so to speak, by implying that God may be ignorant or devoid of intelligence. He begins to "back up" then, hastens to correct himself, and finally even admits (6. 9 (9). 6. 2, 46-50) that, while there is nothing of which the One is cognizant, there is also nothing of which he is ignorant.

It is a delicate balancing act; Plotinus is obviously trying to save *both* types of perfection - transcendence and knowledge - but so far in the Greek tradition the two seem to be in *inverse* relation. For the Greeks, especially in the Platonic tradition, we tend to become "like" what we know; for God to "know" the world, then, would mean for him to be pulled down to its level, to become "like" the world. Thus God's aloofness from, and knowledge of the world would seem to be in inverse proportion and diametrically opposed; they seemingly cannot exist together. Plotinus has chanced upon a device, however, whereby the one may actually *entail* the other; he has thus found a way to transform what appears to be a situation of mutual *exclusion* into one of bi-lateral *inclusion*. In knowing himself adequately or completely (if only through his second hypostasis), God must know all the effects of which he is the necessary cause. This minor comment by Plotinus (it is also suggested by Alexander of Aphrodisias at about the same time) is the revolutionary conceptual device which will allow later thinkers to *pry open* the Aristotelian convention of divine self-knowledge, as a way to resolve the persisting

Greek problem of explaining how God could be self-complete and still produce an independent world. It is a true intellectual breakthrough, because it suggests for the first time a possibility by which these perfections, which before seemed irremediably opposed, may actually be compatible and may coexist. God may not be restricted to *either* knowing himself *or* producing a world, there may be a way to accomodate both, and thus to break this deadlock and impasse which currently besets the Greek philosophical project.

What is true of God is true of everything below him. Plotinus writes:

> What we know as Nature is a Soul, offspring of a yet earlier Soul of more powerful life; it possesses, in its repose, a vision within itself; it has no tendency upward nor downward, but is at peace, steadfast, in its own Essence; in this immutability accompanied by what may be called Self-Consciousness, it possesses a knowledge of the realm of subsequent things perceived in virtue of that understanding and consciousness. 3.8.4

In other words, in knowing itself adequately, Soul simultaneously knows everything that comes *after* it, or is below it. At the level of "Soul," however, an ambiguity enters the cosmic order that is not relevant to the "One" at the top of the order, or the procession within the deity. Soul may turn to recognize its source, or it may turn to attend and become preoccupied with its own effects, or the world of matter below it. (The soul can choose to know the world *directly,* whereas God knows the world *only* indirectly.) This possibility or "swivel" in the thought or contemplation of soul provides the mechanism by which Plotinus can explain both its "fall" *into* the world, and also the possibility of its escape *from* it - that is, it allows the one activity available as an explanatory device (contemplation) to become the mechanism of both the creation *and* the "salvation" (or the "*de*-creation") of the world.

This motif is more clearly spelled out in later Neoplatonic philosophy. A common solution-schema emerges behind the work of several prominent thinkers, including Amelius, Porphyry, Iamblichus, Plutarch, Proclus, and later Islamic philosophy, invoking as its fundamental mechanism the Socratic imperative to "Know Thyself." Now, you can know yourself in various ways or at various levels. If you know yourself only "through yourself" (and thus as just a possible being), you are breaking away in a rebellious bid for autonomy, and thereby produce (or fall down to) the realm of material bodies (below soul). To know yourself "through your cause" or as a necessary being is to know yourself more adequately, to turn to face the source of your being, and thus to contemplate the highest substance. This is the path of conversion, fulfillment, and "salvation" (return to one's source). To know yourself "through yourself," on the contrary, is to attempt an illigitimate imitation of God precisely through the one trait in which we are *not* allowed to imitate him - his independence or self-subsistence; it is to aspire to an unrealistic and inappropriate autonomy, to engage in an apostasy and rebellion against our actual situation (dependence). To attempt this is to pretend that we could be completely or adequately understood through *ourselves* (as only the ultimate substance can be).

However, in knowing ourselves "through ourselves," we simultaneously know all that comes "after" us, all that is implied by our (soul's) nature. On the positive side, this is the source of universal providence, the doctrine that all that happens in the material world is governed as well as produced by soul, or happens at soul's direction. On the negative side, as soul turns now to face what is *below* it, it is in danger of becoming enamored with the specious attractions of the sense world, entangled with its insubstantial glitter, and fatigued in the labors of governing the irrational passions and the chaotic, recalcitrant realm of matter. To turn to face our source is to understand ourselves more adequately (and in proper submission), to pull ourselves back up to the divine level from which we have fallen, and to leave behind the realm of "Nature" (soul-in-matter) - which then presumably dissolves.

As stated, however, an unattractive complication afflicts Plotinus' straightforward application of this cause-and-effect relationship to the godhead. For not only *can* God produce souls and the material world through self-knowledge, on this account he apparently *has* to. Plotinus' account makes matter a necessary side effect of God's nature; the world is definitely not the object of a free choice, or something that God could have failed to bring into being. As such, the world cannot truly be called *distinct* from God, and, as a consequence, Plotinus cannot be said to have explained the apparent independence of the world. In other words, the divine nature has simply *expanded* to *include* the world; we have not led the divine "activity" *beyond* the divine nature itself.

Plotinus cannot bring himself to question the received criterion of divine perfection radically enough to introduce the notion that God could be *interested* in receiving the attention and acknowledgment of beings independent from himself. God is still properly preoccupied exclusively with his *own* nature; the world is simply generated inevitably as a necessary result of his (adequate) self-knowledge. Plotinus has indeed mobilized the considerable resources of the Greek tradition, he has ransacked the storehouse of accumulated ideas from a thousand years of reflection on these topics, he has exploited every possible combination and variation of received notions *short* of challenging the Greek convention of true reality, in a final, all-out assault by a (nearly exhausted) Greek tradition upon the persisting problem of explaining the production of the world. What can be described only as his impressive but flawed performance demonstrates that there is, indeed, a need for a change in that convention and also that anything *short* of this change will simply not do the job - that only this *kind* of a change will allow us to deliver an adequate and finally satisfying account of the world.

But perhaps we are going a bit too fast. Is this impressive failure by Plotinus enough to *justify* us in taking this step? Does a need establish a *fact,* or even beyond that, does it constitute a *proof?* We might say: "Perhaps we *need* a God that is like that; but does that prove that God after all *is* really like that?" When reasoning to a first efficient cause, Aristotle on occasion seems to think that it does; but will *rigor* actually allow us to take this step?

There were specific historical traditions and psychological influences which would make it difficult for followers of the Greek Enlightenment to take this step, to allow for this further, and perhaps necessary change. Even in the wake of the discovered inadequacy of the Plotinian achievement, there would still be considerable resistance and objections from Greek thinkers, chiefly because this change seems to land them back in the *mythic* tradition, characterized by its free and uninhibited indulgence of the imagination, from which these thinkers had been trying to extricate themselves for over a thousand years.[5] "Philosophy" *began* as a reform movement against the excesses of the mythical type of explanation; it called for a purification and heightened discipline, to achieve a more controlled account of the world. Such an expansion of divine perfection would appear to serious thinkers as a capitulation and return to the older, unacceptably fanciful and anthropomorphic legends and stories which the Greek Enlightenment had always criticized, or as a concession and sellout to the new "mystery" cults (or Christianity) which were attracting followers with the promise of an unprecedented and extravagant type of salvation that was, to the sophisticated Greek, pure fastasy, hopelessly out of proportion to man's scale and importance. Perhaps stung by Philo's alternative explanation, Plotinus attempted to mobilize the full resources of the Greek tradition in one final effort to show that one *could* construct an adequate account for the production of the world without having recourse to these flamboyant and romantic innovations, that is, without departing from the orthodox theological tradition of divine perfection at such a fundamental level and in such an objectionable manner. Philosophy had its origin among the myths, to be sure, but at the same time it is essentially a reaction to and cleansing of the myths. By its very existence, it constitutes an *indictment* of the myths, a denial of their adequacy as a final explanation. Any deviation from the central pillar of the Greek philosophical movement - Parmenides' description of "true being" as changeless and self-complete - could not help but strike these thinkers as an abandonment of what was distinctive and valuable in the legacy of Greek philosophy, as a dangerous lapse back into a fairy-tale world of fanciful gods engaging in arbitrary actions, for motives that were, as Nietzsche would later say, "human, all too human." In this regard, it is interesting to note that the phrase "natural theology" or "philosophical theology" was coined not by a Christian apologist distinguishing it from "revealed" or historical theology; on the contrary, it was first used by Varro (a contemporary of Cicero) around 50 B.C.E. to distinguish it from both "poetic" and "civil" theology. The former were the popular myths told about the gods, coming from Homer and his Roman imitators; the latter were beliefs in the festivals and the divine status of the emperor, felt to be necessary to hold the state together. Neither of the latter two were to be trusted, Varro believed; only as purified by "philosophy" could theology be taken seriously.

For those thinkers who will come later and be working within the tradition of a revelation, that is, who believe in a *second* and dramatic initiative by God towards the world, there is, of course, no difficulty in changing this convention; they would have done so anyway, even without the need for it at the purely philosophical level, by reason of their belief. For those who do not work within the context of a revelation, however, this failure of Plotinus' philosophy does indeed make the inadequacy of the received tradition more painfully obvious, and their situation more frustrating; but their attachment to their own convention, and the too-proximate resemblance of this alteration to what they have for so long been trying to avoid, would still give many pause, would make them cautious and hesitant to accept so radical a modification of what they have accepted in the past as an achievement. The establishment of an objective "need," therefore, by no means by itself *guarantees* that the Greek philosophical mind would accept this change. Such a mind may well prefer the "failure" or "inadequacy" of what it sees as its long-established "truth," to the specious attractions of a "solution" or "success" which can be purchased only by capitulating on its most fundamental assumption, by selling out to what it can perceive only as either an illusion or a blasphemy.

Hellenistic culture increasingly stressed the *transcendence* of the One; however, at the same time it also discovered and suggested means (usually non-cognitive) to achieve a *communion* with the godhead, that is, means that served to soften this transcendence and aloofness. Both these tendencies led to a modification of the Parmenidean convention. The neo-Pythagorean philosophers, for example, regularly referred to God as "King" and "Father," and spoke of philosophers receiving "revelations" (traditionally taken as the distinguishing mark of the religious world view in contrast to the philosophic), although they may only mean by this a special insight won by a thinker who had sufficiently purified himself. Plotinus' student Porphery frankly proclaims the goal of philosophy to be "salvation" (*"SOTERIA"*); he was anti-Christian, but he viewed the pagan myths as allegorical representations of philosophical truths (thereby made accessible to the general population). This already constitutes by itself a partial acceptance and rehabilitation of the mythic tradition, a more relaxed attitude than the disdainful attack on all anthropomorphisms which had characterized the earlier stages of Hellenic philosophy. This process goes further still in the later neo-Platonists, such as Iamblichus (320 C.E.) who even proclaims the need for a divine revelation to attain the highest virtue, and puts the priest *ahead* of the philosopher at the summit of his system. Several of his students were active in trying to *re-introduce* the polytheistic cults in Rome. Proclus, living about 470 C.E., claimed to be the recipient of revelations, and also to be the reincarnation of the neo-Pythagorean philosopher Nicomachus. He describes the soul's ascent through the three successive stages of eros, truth, and finally faith; the power of eros moves us to love the beautiful, truth fills us with a knowledge of what can be known; but it is faith that lifts us up to a moment of mystical communion with that which is ineffable and incomprehensible. The emphasis on the *transcendence* of the One (which seemed to place it "beyond knowledge," as well as "beyond Being"), started in Plotinus and increasingly stressed in later neo-Platonic philosophy, besides allowing for a higher type of perfection or "activity" in God, also had the perhaps surprising result of leading philosophers to recognize the need for *another* activity besides knowledge, if true communion with the ultimate source was to take place. The possibility of a movement "both ways" or in both directions was thus opened up. This latter development also softened philosophic objections to forms of discourse which might otherwise be dismissed as "anthropomorphic," for knowledge now had incriminated itself; no objection could be made, for these forms of discourse return to a kind of legitimacy once it is emphasized that we are dealing with a realm "beyond knowledge."[6] Damasius, the last Athenian scholarch before Justinian closed the Platonic Academy, reached the rather startling position that *none* of the philosophic systems had explained how the transcendent "One" produces the world; all the technical terms they employ are only analogies and as such no better than the anthropomorphic terms they were intended to replace. The conclusion he drew was that we should feel as at home using the "anthropomorphic" terms of the myths and superstitions as we do using the supposedly "purified" language of the philosophic systems. The latter enjoys no advantage or superiority over the former. By this stroke, Damasius seems both to recognize the failure of the Aristotelian (and other Greek) philosophical systems to explain the production of the world, and also to soften the prejudice and remove the purely linguistic obstacles separating philosophy from religion, obstacles which before had made any *rapproachement* between the two a delicate and difficult matter. Granted, with Damasius this concession to myth may simply indicate a despair in philosophy, and may also go too far, for we are in danger of losing any control whatever over the mythic "explanations." Thus this does not by itself necessarily represent a change in the traditional Greek notion of God. However, these are signs that the poverty of the alternative theoretical possibilities was pushing some thinkers to a further, radical modification of the idea of God - even those who did not accept purported revelations. Hierocles of Alexandria, for example, who lectured there around 430 C.E., rejected the neo-Platonic emanation theory of his intellectual forebeares and specified instead that the Demiurge creates the world *voluntarily* and out of nothing. The world is eternal (was not created in time), but is still the result of a *free act* by the Demiurge, as opposed to being a necessary consequence of his nature.

However, given the weight and prestige of the Parmenidean tradition, it is not surprising that this change did *not* take place as a major cultural phenomena until these problems were taken up by thinkers working within the tradition of a revelation - Jewish, Islamic, or Christian - that is, where the convention of Parmenides is already (and for "outside" reasons) decisively broken or expanded. The different set of assumptions of this latter group of thinkers predispose them to accept this new hypothesis at the outset and to apply it to the problem of explaining the production of the physical world; their belief will allow them to explore and expand the clue Plotinus had thrown out about how God's self-knowledge may not exclude, but may rather *involve* the knowledge of other beings, with fewer inhibitions; it will free them to embrace actively the notion that Plotinus was perhaps backing slowly into because of the poverty of any alternative hypothesis, but which he could not, in the final analysis, accept.[7]

Plotinus is the central figure and true turning point in this process because, besides suggesting that God might be "infinite," and thus deeper than form, his new conceptual device constitutes the intellectual breakthrough that would be developed by later thinkers to explain how God could produce the world simply in knowing himself. The limitation of divine activity to *self*-contemplation, in fact, constitutes the major stumbling block, and the biggest "scandal," of the Aristotelian philosophy for later Jewish, Islamic, and Christian thinkers - a more serious obstacle than even the eternity of the world; for the latter hypothesis, even if true, is not necessarily opposed to faith (as both Maimonides and Thomas Aquinas assert, God could have chosen to create the world from all eternity). On the other hand, the necessary self-contemplation of God *does* appear threatening, perhaps even fatal to faith, because it seems to deny even the *possibility* of a revelation - that God could take an interest in anything *beyond* himself - not to mention making it impossible for God to produce an independent world. That is, this description by Aristotle seems to deny the very possibility, to pull the rug definitively out from under faith in a *revealing* deity. We should notice, incidently, that on the level of theology these two theses - creation and revelation - have the same status or make substantially the same claim about God: they both demand an initiative on God's part, that God should be able to move *outside* himself, towards something meaningfully "other" than himself. They are thus equally shocking or objectionable from an Aristotelian point of view (and, we might add, *vice versa*). Revelation is no more shocking than creation in this regard; and on the other hand, creation is every bit as scandalous and objectionable as revelation. Creation only *seems* more "natural" and hence acceptable, because an account of its source is thought to be a necessary part of any finally adequate explanation of the physical world; a theory of revelation, by contrast, strikes us as "gravy" - that is, as extraneous, otherworldly, strictly speaking irrelevant, and hence dispensable in a satisfactory account of the natural world.

In this regard, it might be illuminating and helpful to suggest that, although Aristotle's philosophy is deficient in not having an account of "creation," he *can* be said to have a rather elaborate and sophisticated theory of "salvation," albeit of a natural variety - of salvation defined as meaningfull satisfaction, or as a means to instill a sense of worth in our condition. Unfortunately, however, this theory of salvation is jeopardized and undercut precisely by his inability to provide an account for the production of an independent world. This absence compromises the *quality* of the contemplative experience he can offer us, and thus renders questionable his claim to have pointed out an inherently valuable activity, excellence, or natural "salvation" available for humanity.

In his ethical writings, Aristotle devotes considerable attention to a discussion of how man may bestow value, excellence, and meaning upon his condition; the reason we may call this discussion a theory of "natural salvation" is that he explicitly claims that happiness is achieved by man's imitating, approximating, and eventually *uniting* with the "pure activity" of the godhead as closely as he can; surely no advocate of a revealed religion could find anything to criticize in this as a definition of "salvation." Aristotle writes in the **Nicomachean Ethics**, "The gods enjoy a life blessed in its entirety; men enjoy it to the extent that they attain something resembling the divine activity." (1178b 26)

He expands on this theme in ch. 7 of book 10 of the same work:

> A man who would live (a contemplative life) would do so not insofar as he is human, but because there is a divine element within him. This divine element is as far above our composite nature as its activity is above the active exercise of the other (i.e., practical) kind of virtue. So if it is true that intelligence is divine in comparison with man, then a life guided by intelligence is divine in comparison with human life. . . We should try to become immortal as far as that is possible and do our utmost to live in accordance with what is highest in us. For though this is a small portion (of our nature), it far surpasses everything else in power and value. One might even regard it as each man's true self, since it is the controlling and better part. (1177b 27-1178a 2; tr. Ostwald)

Of course, what distinguishes Aristotle's salvation from that associated with revealed religion is that no claim is made that God takes any initiative towards humanity; in fact, quite the contrary, this possibility is emphatically denied. Nevertheless, and regardless of how we may have got here - "cast up upon this alien shore," as Matthew Arnold puts it - Aristotle is under no illusion but that the *only* way we may introduce value into our lives now is to imitate and approximate God's condition as closely as possible. This does not necessarily involve a monastic withdrawal and worldly renunciation, however; we do so through our normal activities, when they are carried out and cultivated to a state of "excellence"; but the reason they are virtuous, finally (because they are all the realization or "actualization" of a potentiality), is that they allow us to imitate and share more fully in the "pure activity" (or "perfect excellence") that *is* and defines God. Also, as stated, all the effort must come from "our" side; it is an entirely "Pelagian" brand of salvation - all work on our part, and no special grace from God. We try to get as close to God as we can, *he* does not (and cannot) try to come close to us. Such would lower his perfection and, indeed, compromise his very divinity. Fortunately, once that limitation is accepted, Aristotle feels that we are living in the dispensation of a comparatively benign deity. For all nature is now trying to imitate God, so that ethics can *build upon* and tap into these primeval energies, rather than having to fight to overcome them. The progression of motion in the individual's development is from the comparative chaos of matter towards the progressive realization of *form,* which is, in its own way, already a turning back and an imitation of the "pure form" of the absolute substance. Thus, *each* act of "motion" or development can be said to be characterized by the twin moments of outflow and return, rebellion and conversion, apostasy and repentance, which Plotinus later made *constitutive* of the very being of the individual; it is not difficult to see how these elements form a natural outgrowth of Aristotle's analysis of motion. And Plotinus' philosophy, although it describes a God which, if anything, is even *more* transcendent and aloof than Aristotle's, is conceived primarily and explicitly as a manual for personal *salvation,* that is, as a means to effect a conversion, a return, and a final merging of the individual with the "One," based on an ascent through his knowledge and love of higher objects.[8]

Thus, Aristotle gives us a fairly optimistic description of this God in whose dispensation we happen to be living. The goal of moral education is to cultivate virtue or excellence. For Aristotle, virtue is not painful or difficult to acquire, because it is fortunately the case that our bodies are so constituted that *pleasure* tends to accompany (or "kick in") whenever our capacities are used properly or with excellence; this pleasure then tends to reinforce and support us in this "excellent" activity. Thus, the entire cosmos conspires to lead us towards our natural goal, the "end" or *"TELOS"* of our development. Of course, it did not *have* to be this way; in this sense, the deity we are living under can be said to be benign or well-disposed towards us. Pleasure - at least the "natural" pleasure specific to each activity done with skill - is a *good* for us, not evil; training in virtue works *with* nature rather than against it, bringing it simply and straight-forwardly to its immanent perfection. All seems suited, therefore, to lead us "naturally" and as painlessly as possible to this highest goal, our true end ("form"), and thereby to imitate God (who is "pure form"). Pleasure can even lift us momentarily "out of time," and thus allow what is "most divine" in each one of us temporarily to escape the sub-lunar realm and to rejoin, momentarily, its ultimate source.

And what *is* the highest activity for Aristotle? It can only be the activity that is distinctive to man, which only he can perform; and that, for Aristotle, is thinking or contemplation. Man is privileged to be able to engage in the same sort of activity as God - thinking - and he can direct this activity to the same object, God himself, which is where the greatest excellence (and hence our highest pleasure) are to be experienced. It is when we are achieving excellence in this activity that our resemblance to, and imitation of, God becomes most complete - that is, by the "identity of indiscernibles" and our inability to specify a difference between ourselves and God (matter, as a principle of "otherness" or individuation, falls away, as we become "non-other" from God), the possibility of a return to and even mystical fusion with the godhead becomes theoreti-cally possible.[9]

This process can be described as a "natural salvation"; it is "natural" because it is brought about entirely by ourselves and requires no special intervention by God. It is a "salvation," both in the general sense of conferring meaning, value, and the highest satisfaction upon our exis-tence, and in the more precise sense of achieving *union* with God. It is also the capstone of the arch of the Aristotelian philosophy, the point of union between practical and theoretical virtue, the goal towards which all nature is aspiring, as it strains through us to rejoin its source, from which it has mysteriously fallen and been tragically exiled.

But it is precisely here, in his account of contemplation, that

Aristotle's theory of salvation breaks down; specifically, it is his failure
to provide a theory for the production of the world that is its undoing. The
content of this "contemplation" is never spelled out, beyond saying that
it is of the highest object; but presumably, if this "first substance" is
known adequately, our contemplation must progress to some account of
how the various subordinate substances have emerged as distinct beings
from the highest substance; otherwise it would not be a "complete"
knowledge, would not attain its distinctive excellence or virtue, and
would presumably not be accompanied by its characteristic pleasure. But
this is precisely what happens. Aristotle *has no* account of how lower
substance emerges from the highest separate substance; indeed, not only
does he have no account, on his theory this emergence seems *impossible*.
This result, however, has more than casual significance for his theory of
"natural salvation." It means, specifically, that our contemplation can
never be "complete" or satisfactory; rather, it must always be impeded,
difficult, characterized by friction, and thus void of its distinctive pleasure. The deity whose dispensation was imagined so positively may not
be as benign as we were at first led to believe. "Contemplation" is a
promisory note in Aristotelian philosophy, which is never filled in or
redeemed. It is like the vision of "the Good" which Plato's philosopher
supposedly receives at the highest level of the divided line; we are told
that it exists, but we are never given a full account of its content, of *how*
it is good - specifically of how the first being "overspills" itself to produce
the world. Aristotle's three theoretical sciences (physics, mathematics,
and metaphysics or "first philosophy") are supposed to supply us with the
content of the full theoretical vision which it is possible for us to attain in
these three areas of inquiry. His failure to *deliver* an account of how first
substance produces lower substance, indeed, his apparent demonstration
that such a production is *impossible,* erodes and severely compromises
his theory of contemplation as an inherently satisfying activity; indeed,
it redounds and reflects negatively upon his ethics and philosophy as a
whole, it shows that, at least at its highest levels, this ethical theory is
deceptive and a fraud. Excellence in the theoretical activity is apparently
not available to us; at least Aristotle himself has failed to produce a
convincing specimen. As a consequence, in attempting to make our life
satisfactory, we must seek our pleasures where we may find them, at
lower levels apparently, since they are not available here. This may
involve eventually cauterizing or excising our speculative faculty entirely (as the modern Enlightenment opted to do); the pain involved in that

operation may still be less than the persisting frustration of not being able to satisfy our natural and legitimate theoretical curiosity. This result also removes contemplation from being a "salvation" in any serious sense, since the attempt to cultivate this activity leads only to pain and frustration, which cannot (and should not) be tolerated for long. It turns out that we cannot get "close" to God after all through contemplation. Or perhaps we can; but then, why should we? Or who would (now) want to? For what this result really does is to *indict* the God who put us in such a condition in the first place, one who would equip us with a theoretical interest and curiosity which in principle cannot be satisfied. This highest substance appears now in an altogether different light, as an ambiguous and possibly malicious entity who delights in setting us up with rational desires that can only make our life (and the condition of nature straining beneath and through us) one of inherent futility and inevitable, prolonged frustration. Not only is God transcendent and aloof, he is apparently playing a bad joke upon us - one which, in the end, only he can enjoy.

Salvation plays an essential role when we approach Aristotle's theory "from above," as well as "from below"; it supplies a necessary step when we come to the question of what *motive* could possibly have led God to produce a world in the first place. Without salvation - understood as the call to relationship with God - creation or the production of the world becomes an arbitrary, and perhaps an ultimately irrational growth within the cosmic pattern. And from our point of view as well (that is, apart from God's motivation), if we are denied the satisfaction (a kind of "natural salvation") of *understanding* our world, at least to some extent - if we are denied the sense of depending upon and subsisting within the context of an ultimately *rational* agency - then the value of "creation," or our existence here, again becomes uncertain and questionable. Natural existence, then, is not simply a neutral reality, always the same, but rather takes on a positive or negative coloring, a good or bad "flavor," depending upon what sort of "salvation" (or excellence) we believe is available through it and for it. If there is absolutely no salvation in this broad sense, no understanding or intellectual satisfaction possible in the world, then what we call "creation" becomes gratuitous, an uncaused protuberance, without why or wherefore, an arbitrary, uncontrolled, and indeed cancerous growth in the logical pattern of the cosmos, prompting an appropriate rational response of disgust, nausea, and final rejection. The surprising result that develops within our investigation, then, is that creation itself will require some moment of "redemption" - that is, an account by which the source of existence desires to be known and appreciated by beings other than itself - for creation *itself* to become for the first time intelligible, or to be rescued from final irrationality. Strangely enough, then, "natural" forces will require us to posit a transcendent *initiative,* or a softening of the Parmenidean convention, at the levels of both "creation" and "salvation," in the sense that "nature" otherwise falls into absurdity.

Creation, or the world, is "first known" in the order of time; but in the order of explanation, it is *salvation* that comes first as supplying God's *motive* in producing a world, that is, which conditions and makes creation first possible. From the divine point of view, creation and salvation are not completely separable, but are better viewed as two moments of a single divine initiative and desire to communicate itself. Each implies and requires the other; neither can stand alone, although both initially seem able to. It is our mistake to separate creation and salvation as two complete and isolatable events. In reality, they go together naturally and require one another, as in a two-beat syncopation. Creation is essential as making "salvation" (as friendship or fulfillment) possible; and salvation is only the completion, the bringing to term, of what was begun at creation. Salvation without creation would perhaps be appropriate to demi-gods or angels (or Aristotle's forty-four "unmoved movers"); creation (of rational creatures) without some form of salvation would be an appropriate punishment only for devils.

Thus, the final result of the historical dialectic is this: a theory of creation or the production of the world through efficient causality is necessary to explain the world, or to render Aristotle's system complete. This is what Plotinus' philosophy (and Greek philosophy as a whole) lacked. But, *given* creation or the free production of an independent world, a theory of *salvation* is necessary to make creation *itself* for the first time rational. New needs are discovered with each new breakthrough or "solution," until at last, with "salvation," the force of "negativity" (as Hegel calls it) runs its course and exhausts itself; no further postulates need to be made. Our explanation is, as far as it can be, complete. Of course, what *form* this salvation is going to take is not at this point clear; as a notion, it is still vague and unspecified. It is certainly not to be identified necessarily or without further ado with any one historical figure, such as Moses or Jesus. At the same time, it is no accident that this development, this softening of the Parmenidean convention of divine perfection, occurred almost exclusively among groups which believed in a divine revelation; they were the only ones sufficiently sensitized to this hypothesis of a higher type of perfection in God to overcome the scruples Greek philosophy held against such a change, and to apply it to the on-going and outstanding deficiency within Greek philosophy. But in and of itself, what this "salvation" will look like is, and must remain at the philosophical level, a mystery. What does seem essential is that we must be able to enter into *some* sort of relationship with the deity, characterized by mutual recognition and friendship, as far as this is possible. Without this as its end and goal, we have discovered, the production of the world is equivocal, makes no sense, and has no particular value. Without salvation (understood in this broad sense), creation becomes *irrational*. Thus, given creation, redemption is virtually "necessary," that is, dictated or implied by the data. Not only has salvation, then, been shown to be *compatible* with a philosophical explanation of nature; it has been discovered, to our surprise perhaps, that is is in some sense called for or required if one is to give a finally adequate account of the natural world.

NOTES

1   See Ch. II, ftn. 4.

2   See Norris Clarke, "The Limitation of Act By Potency," **NEW SCHOLASTICISM**, Vol. 26, Apr. '52, pp. 167-94.

3   See Plotinus, **Enneads**, 5.4 (7), Ch. 1, II. 26-41, 5.1 (10), Ch. 6, I. 37, 5.2 (11), Ch. 1, I. 8

4   In the Plotinian system, Soul is the (third) hypostasis which intro-duces Forms into Matter, thus bringing into being "Nature," or the world we see around us. The "One" produces *"Nous"* as the (finite) image of itself. *Nous* turns toward the One and contemplates it, thereby producing Soul, which turns towards its source, until the last emanation is produced, Matter. In 4.8.3, 21 ff., Plotinus explains the "creation" of the world of Nature, or the organized world of Forms-in-Matter. When Soul knows itself through its *source*, it stays at the level of *Nous*, or *returns* there if it is below; this is the avenue of "salvation" in the Plotinian system. When Soul knows itself through *itself*, it knows simultaneously what comes *after* it, and descends to that level, where it introduces the Forms into Matter, thereby direct-

ing and governing this world. This is the avenue of "creation" within
the Plotinian system. See J.M. Rist, **Plotinus: the Road to Reality**,
Cambridge Univ. Pr., N.Y., 1967, ch. 7, esp. pp. 89-90.

Thus there is primordially a great gulf fixed between Soul and
Matter; the situation is similar to that described at the beginning of
Genesis: "In the beginning God created the heavens and the earth.
The earth was without form and void, and darkness was upon the face
of the deep." **(Revised Standard Version)** "Nature" as we know it
did not yet exist. Soul generously tries to rescue or "redeem" Matter
from total chaos, by descending and introducing Forms into it; but for
that Soul pays the price of becoming preoccupied and enmeshed with
material things itself, and thus of descending from its proper condition of contemplating Nous.

Matter's redemption is Soul's perdition. Although generous on
Soul's part, this ambition to "rescue" Matter is inherently futile, since
there seems to be a fixed limit as to how far Matter can be organized
or "lifted up" by Form. Matter cannot be "redeemed" beyond the
level of "Nature." Plotinus seems eventually to have decided that the
cost of attaining this limited salvation is too great; the descent of Soul
should never have taken place. Soul's "salvation" will consist in its
turning back to contemplate its source in *Nous;* at that time it will
reascend to its previous level, "Nature" will presumably go out of
existence, and Matter will return to its original disorganized state.
The first three hypostases turn to contemplate their source spontaneously, or of their own; Matter, however, needs Soul to introduce Form
into it (as far as this is possible). Soul therefore becomes the one
exception to the general Greek convention of perfection, whereby the
higher never inclines to take account of the lower, but rather the lower
always turns or "converts" to acknowledge and contemplate the
higher. However, the result is not worth the price, as far as Soul is
concerned. Plotinus seems to conclude that the project, although
laudable, was inherently hopeless, and should never have been
attempted in the first place. There is no *"redditus"* of the world to
God, because Matter cannot be lifted up to the divine level. Soul must
give up its ambition to redeem the world, and return to its celestial
home alone. The "last" state of the world (when Soul is converted or
has "saved" itself) will be like its first. This is, obviously, very close
to the Gnostic outlook, although Plotinus tried to stop short of their
position.

5　At **MET** 983a 2, Aristotle refers to Plato's statement that the gods cannot be jealous (**Timaeus** 42E 5-6, **Phaedrus** 247A) and adds wryly the proverb "For bards tell many a lie." At **Enneads** 2.9.22, 21 Plotinus criticizes those who imagine that Soul created Matter in order to gain glory; on the contrary, he emphasizes, this is only an anthropomorphic way of conceiving the divine activity. Apparently, a "purified" explanation requires discussion and speculation on God's motivation in producing the world.

Aristotle gives a good indication of the "flavor" of the Greek Enlightenment, in contrast to the 18th-Century Enlightenment, by such statements as the following:

The ancients of very early times bequeathed to posterity in the form of a myth a tradition that the heavenly bodies are gods and that the divinity encompasses the whole of nature. The rest of the tradition has been added later as a means of persuading the masses and as something useful for the laws and for matters of expediency; for they say that these gods are like men in form and like some of the other animals, and also other things which follow from or are similar to those stated. But if one were to separate from the later additions the first point and attend to this alone (namely, that they thought the first substances to be gods), he might realize that this was divinely spoken and that, while probably every art and every philosophy has often reached a stage of development as far as it could and then has perished, these doctrines about the gods were saved like relics up to the present day. Anyway, the opinion of our forefathers and of the earliest thinkers is evident to us to just this extent.

MET 1074b 1-14

6　Zeller himself was not able to overcome his allegiance to the Parmenidean convention of divine perfection; on the contrary, he sees any affiliation and fusion with religion as the extinction of true philosophy. In a sense, and ironically, the modern 18th-century Enlightenment is more faithful or inflexible in the observance of this Parmenidean convention than was the first or Greek Enlightenment. Perhaps this comes from the fact that the modern Enlightenment arose after the spread of Christianity, to which it was reacting as an oppressive anthropomorphic ideology. Zeller writes:

The neo-Platonists doubted in the last instance the possibility of theoretical knowledge of the ultimate basis of all being and sought a remedy in revelation received in a state of mystical ecstasy. . . Thus neo-Platonism with its need of revelation instead of independent investigation carried to its end the development begun in neo-Pythagoreanism and the Greek-Jewish philosophy and thus completed the suicide of philosophy. Only the fact that the liberation from the bonds of the sensual is a self-liberation which the philosopher can accomplish with his own strength remains the last flickering of the splendor of the Socratic *"autarkia."*

Outlines of the History of Greek Philosophy, Dover, N.Y., 1980 (tr. Palmer), p. 290.

7   These thinkers were predisposed towards what turns out to be a helpful and needed hypothesis about the divine nature, not through any special "content" of their revelation, but because of what they took revelation itself to *be:* God *could* take an initiative towards the world, because he evidently *had.*   That is, it was not any specific *content* of their revelation which gave them a special help in solving the problem of explaining the production of the world (as if God told them "how he did it"). Rather, their belief in the reality of revelation itself focused their attention upon the central assumption of Greek philosophy which denied the possibility of a revelation - and which also, as it happened, needed to be modified if Greek philosophy was to develop a successful explanation of the production of the world. In a sense, therefore, it is an historical accident or coincidence that this alteration meets the outstanding need in Greek philosophy; the later thinkers working under the conviction of a revelation would probably have made the change anyway, even if there had been no particular need. Still, it is surprisingly useful in enabling the Greek project to achieve its own end.

8   Plotinus expands the Socratic maxim "Know Thyself" into a practical method of salvation, or return to the One.   To "know" yourself adequately is to relate yourself to your highest cause. This knowledge does not leave you unchanged, for as Aristotle says, in knowledge the knower somehow becomes *one* with the object known. Thus, to turn and "know" our highest cause is already somehow to lift ourselves "up," to escape our normal condition of imprisonment in illusion, to return to and rejoin the cause (or origin) from which we have mysteriously fallen. Thus, knowledge by itself is sufficient to effect

this "translation" of the soul; and "salvation" is simply the reversal of creation; it cancels and erases the mistake that constituted the production of the world.

9   **Nicomachean Ethics,** Bk. 10, chs. 7 & 8. This is also why God coincides with his own thought. The first substance is immaterial. But "thought" retains the form while leaving behind whatever is material. Thus God, in thinking himself, is indiscernibly different from the thought of himself; or his thought perfectly coincides with his self, without diminution or remainder. Thus God is well described as "thought thinking itself."

CHAPTER FOUR

THE RATIONALIST PARADIGM

In the period after Aristotle, Greek theorists experimented with various ways of combining Plato's (productive) theology and Aristotle's theory of divine self-contemplation; that is, ways of retaining Parmenides' convention of perfection while still explaining the production of the world.[1] Some were, perhaps, stung by Philo the Jew's bold assertion of the free creation of the world by God (around 50 C.E.), to expend more effort to come up with their own counter-explanation, for the Greeks generally could not accept the doctrine of a free creation. From their point of view, the uncritical acceptance of this device would constitute a relapse into mythic and anthropomorphic thinking, from which they were struggling to escape. Also, for a Hellenistic Greek, no god could touch matter, and still remain god. That is why they were so opposed to the Christian doctrine of the Incarnation (and why the Greek church stressed it so much, almost at times seeming to suggest that salvation comes primarily through the Incarnation, independent of what transpired later in the life of Jesus. Irenaeus of Lyons (c. 180 C.E.), perhaps the first systematic Christian thinker, in his **Refutation and Overthrow of Knowledge falsely so called,** presented the Incarnation as the infusion of divine substance into human existence, which is then extended through the sacraments as the agency of salvation.) The Son of God must have actually taken on a human nature, and not just been a God who "appeared" as human, as the Christian Gnostics asserted; as the pithy statement of the later Greek fathers put it, "what has not been taken on, is not redeemed." Athanasius writes (c. 350 C.E.):

By taking our nature and offering it in sacrifice, the Word was to destroy it completely and then invest it with his own nature, and so prompt the Apostle to say: "This corruptible body must put on incorruption; this mortal body must put on immortality." . . . Man's body has acquired something great through its communion and union with the Word. From being mortal it has been made immortal; though it was a living body it has become a spiritual one; though it was made from the earth it has passed through the gates of heaven. **Epist. ad Epictetum** 5-9 **P.G.** 26, 1058-1066

The Greek emphasis on the gulf between God and matter led the fathers to stress this "kenotic" (condescending or self-emptying) interpretation of salvation, as contrasted with the "suffering" or "atonement" theory represented in later Western works such as Anselm's **Cur Deus Homo**. For a Hellenistic Greek, the material world is the lowest and most distant emanation from the "One"; it is equivalent to non-existence, is close to stepping over the line and becoming positively evil. The Gnostics actually took this step; Plotinus vacillates, but eventually announces his opposition to the Gnostic view. Not only is the Incarnation ruled out for a Greek, but for the same reason direct or free creation. There must be a series of intermediaries, or buffers, placed between the world and God, and the world must be produced unconsciously. For God to care about the world and to have direct, unmediated contact with it would be to lower himself to its level. Knowledge has a metaphysical power for the Greek. It lifts the knower up or down to the level of the object to which he is attending. Thus the Greek theorists have to be careful about which objects they allow their God actively to "know." God must only contemplate *himself,* if he is to stay perfectly God; and insofar as we humans "convert" and turn our gaze to God also, we rise to his level and rejoin the source from which we have tragically fallen or been mysteriously separated.[2] "Salvation" is possible through the autonomous power of knowledge; this is fortunate for us, because it is the only power at our disposal. God cannot take a step towards us. And what "salvation" consists in is reversing the cosmic mistake that was creation.

In the interests of filling the omission in Aristotle, or in developing a counter-explanation to Philo, the Middle Platonists experimented with putting Plato's "Forms" as "Ideas" into the Aristotelian "Mind" of God. The only activity God can be allowed is contemplation - indeed, *self-*contemplation. Therefore, if the world is to be explained, somehow this self-contemplation by God has to be made productive, for that is the only device they had to work with. By putting the "Forms" of all things directly into the Mind of God, the problem is in its essentials solved, because in knowing himself, God can be said to know simultaneously all things, at least indirectly, as his potential effects or consequences. This is the only shape that a solution *could* take, drawing upon traditional Greek resources. This move, which seems rather obvious to us, was slow to dawn or be accepted by Greek theorists, however; it developed only slowly over several hundred years. For what really is required is not just insight, but the softening of the Parmenidean resistance to the notion that God could be in any way active towards a (distinct) world. It required a change in attitude and a gathering of interest in the problem of explaining the production of the physical world, and an openness to whatever hypothesis is found necessary to achieve this. Before Greek theorists could accept the *further* "device" of a free creation, they would have to exhaust the resources they were familiar with, to see if they could not come up with something less dramatic that could do the same job. This was an essential first step, therefore, before they would accept the notion of a free creation, voluntarily if relunctantly.

The preferred Greek solution of a necessary but unconscious or unintended emanation of the world from God lands us very close to the Gnostic position, which views the world of matter as a low and un-trustworthy "shadow-realm," attractive in its glitter but ultimately unsub-stantial, and so distant from the realm of "true Being" (the Forms) that it cannot be "known" in a strict sense at all. By contrast (and by working backwards), the hypothetical realm of "true Being" is invested with precisely the qualities of sameness, stability, regularity, and necessity which from Plato onwards the Greek tradition has viewed as the hall-marks of reality and trustworthy knowledge. If one suspects that one is living in a world of irregular, insubstantial, and possibly evil matter, where any *apparent* order may be a trap set to mislead and deceive us, then the only order which one should trust is the strict necessity which characterizes the "higher" realm, where consequences follow from prem-ises immediately and with full deductive rigor. Analogously, the only paradigm of explanation which we should accept is that of strict causality understood as necessary connection, with only *univocal* predication tolerated, as in a mathematical deduction. Nothing else can be counted on as reliably certain. Aristotle had tried to soften this paradigm, to allow for analogous language to describe the higher realities, or "separate substances"; but later Hellenistic thinkers saw themselves as living in a less stable universe than Aristotle had imagined, where no apparent order could be accepted at face value and no civil institution could simply be taken for granted. As a consequence, they retreated in practice to a position close to Plato's (who had also made significant concessions to the Sophists' view of the *flux* of the sensible world), and espoused his ideal of a fully purged, mathematical clarity, as the characteristic trait of the highest (and only trustworthy) form of knowledge, a knowledge which can lift us *beyond* this insubstantial and shadowy realm, a knowledge which can actually attain stable objects and thus bring us relief from our "this-worldly" psychological anxieties. From this sceptical methodological posture, only *necessary* causes are to be respected as true causes, only fully determined effects can be trusted to be reliably effects. The goal in this pursuit of knowledge is that of a fully purified, non-mythological explanation that will satisfy the highest ideals of the Greek Enlightenment. Any object which cannot adapt or conform to this paradigm cannot become an object of scientific knowledge, cannot be truly "known" at all; and any account which does not live up to these rigorous standards of explanation should be distrusted.

Socrates, of course, lets himself off the hook from delivering a fuller account of this level, by calling himself a "philosopher" - someone who "loves" or is seeking knowledge, without having as yet attained it. Thus he does not claim to be at the fourth level himself - in fact, quite the contrary. In the seemingly artless craftsmanship of the dialogues, Socrates is depicted as merely reporting to us something he has heard about or believes in, rather than something he has experienced directly. We may credit this simply to a false modesty; but it may also be a shrewd ploy by Plato, used strategically to excuse himself from having to deliver a fuller account of something he says exists but is never able himself to describe in non-mythological terms.

This ideal of a fully purged or rational explanation is never achieved in the Greek tradition. Theorists continue to pursue and swear allegiance to it, however, and to look upon any explanation which falls short of it with askance, as if it were to that extent inadequate, unacceptable, and a cause for embarrassment. Now, it is obvious that the motif of the free creation of the world, proclaimed by Philo, is not amenable to expression in this format. If the world is truly independent of God, then it does not follow necessarily from God's nature, and it cannot be expressed as a necessary consequence of his essence or form. The only way Plotinus can solve the *aporia* of the Aristotelian philosophy, to explain how God, as self-thinking *"NOUS,"* can also produce the world, is to place the ideas of things in God's mind where he knows them as necessary consequences of his own nature. This allows the world to be generated, but it is now a fully determined side-effect of his own being; in other words, its independence is compromised. This is hardly a better explanation than we had with Aristotle. God has merely expanded to absorb the world, or the world has been "collapsed back" into God.

But, if Greek philosophy may be depicted as "backing into" an account of the *free creation* of the world by God, merely to escape the inadequacies which seem to afflict every *other* attempt to solve this problem, how can this account escape the strictures and criticism to which earlier "mythological" accounts were vulnerable? For how far may we relax our criteria of divine perfection *safely*, without falling back into uncontrollably imaginative accounts, escapist fantasies, or merely wishful thinking? This is the dilemma which after Plotinus confronts and paralyzes the Greek Enlightenment, stopped at the crossroads where it feels the inadequacy of its present position, but also unsure as to how and in which direction it may properly proceed.[3] In "expanding" the traditional convention of divine perfection, whose inadequacy has been sufficiently demonstrated, are we not in danger of relaxing our criteria of "explanation" unacceptably, down to the level of mere "story"?[4] If so, what defense do we have against an excessive accomodation to the imagination and senses - which admittedly constitute the only level the masses can understand? If it is true that our account of God must somehow become more dynamic or "personalized," what will keep us from going too far and falling headlong into pure mythology? What is to count now as an adequate and yet nonetheless "rational" explanation?

This bias against any account which makes concessions to the senses and the imagination (and the correlative goal of a totally necessary, or strictly deductive explanation), continued to be felt for several hundred years, even among "people of the book," that is, thinkers working within the tradition of a direct revelation by God. Philo himself begins a long tradition of accomodating revealed scriptures with the results of the Greek Enlightenment. For example, in acknowledging the philosophical point that God is non-corporeal and cannot be said to "move," he distinguishes two senses in the Hebrew scriptures, one higher and non-anthropological, and the other lower and anthropological, suited to ordinary people. Although he asserts that the same truths are found in both Greek philosophy and the scriptures, and even suggests that the Greek thinkers may have gotten some of their ideas from reading the Hebrew scriptures, in practice Philo tends to play down the special initiative by God described in the the Bible. Rather, the *transcendence* of God is stressed, and he creates the world not directly, but through a series of intermediary beings, the highest of which is *LOGOS* (the place of the

Forms). While the law of the Torah should always be obeyed, Philo says, true ethical virtue consists in "likeness to God," which is specified in Socratic fashion as the care of the soul, leading for Philo to a weakening and apathy of the passions, and finally to a passive ecstasy. In a similar way, Clement and Origen in Alexandria, around 200 C.E., distinguish two types of Christianity, the first and lower type based on "faith" and a rather literal interpretation of scriptures, the second and higher type based on *"GNOSIS,"* where one has plunged more deeply into the central mysteries. Similarly, Clement claims Jesus Christ was "passionless", a description which represents the triumph of the Parmenidean convention of divine perfection over the Judeo-Christian expansion of that convention, rather than the reverse. Augustine, around 400 C.E., postponed entering the Catholic Church for over ten years, partly because he felt it held an excessively anthropomorphic view of God. In the **De Libero Arbitrio** he argues that we must come to an understanding of God as bodiless and non-temporal, for these are, for Augustine, the characteristics of *"vere esse"* - "true being." At that time this view was not universally shared in the Christian church; Tertullian, for example, held that God was material. Origen was the first to argue, for philosophical reasons, that God must be conceived as immaterial. Finally, even as late as 1277, among the propositions circulating among the Arts faculty of the University of Paris that were condemned by Bishop Tempier, were the following: "that there is no more excellent state than to devote oneself to philosophy," and that "the wise men of the world are the philosophers alone." Christian scriptures were being challenged by the world view contained in the Aristotelian texts, spreading for the first time throughout the West. Apparently some professors on the Arts faculty (such as Boethius of Dacia) suggested as a way of handling their apparent contradiction with the scriptural world view the development of a second, non-literal interpretation of scripture, one that would make it compatible with the independent, philosophical (Aristotelian) view of the world; and the philosophical interpretation would be held to be the "truer" (non-imaginary) account of the same reality. This recourse of accomodation thus seems to be a recurring option to this problem. But the historical point is that, even among "people of the book," for many centuries it was not "understanding" which expanded to accept the promptings of "faith," but rather faith which *contracted* to conform to the limitations enforced by an anxiety-ridden and mathematically impressed "understanding."

The early Middle Ages are characterized by an uncritical homage to an ideal of "rational explanation" that aspires to the sort of logical deductive rigor that characterizes Euclidean geometry: that is, one where basic principles are "self-evidently true," and from which proceed a chain of reasoning which is strictly necessary and that establishes its conclusions with full deductive rigor. The reason for the seductive appeal of this model is not difficult to discover. Not only is this method guaranteed to keep us from falling into error and deception; but anyone who has had a high school course in geometry knows the pleasure, after spending hours trying to prove a theorem to no avail, of having the solution suddenly "pop" into one`s mind, so that one has a mild version of the "Eureka" experience of Archimedes in the bathtub. Theologians in both the Islamic and Christian worlds, interested in discovering effective means to convert educated pagans to their respective faiths, were attracted to the possibility of finding "necessary" or "compelling" reasons for articles which first had to be accepted on faith alone. If such "necessary reasons" (as Augustine called them) could be discovered, an analogous Archimedean pleasure could be generated and tapped in this *theological* area, and it would be easier to demonstrate to potential converts the inherent reasonableness of their respective faiths. Several of these theologians also followed this seductive attraction to the next level, to claim that once one had taken the step "up" to reason, the help given by the "ladder" of faith could be safely dispensed with, and the "ladder" itself kicked down, with the result that reason could completely *replace* faith. The masses, as Averroes states, may never be able to accomplish this second step, and it is for them that the scriptures have been given in a deliberately imaginative and pictorial form, so as to be accessible to all. But for the gifted elite who could rise to the level of purely rational apprehension, the aid of faith could be dispensed with safely, after one has made the ascent. Thus the older Ionian disdain for the masses, the Greek program to cleanse the myths of their unworthy anthropomorphic elements, the Platonic suspicion and distrust of any supposed "truths" still wrapped in a sensuous or imaginative garb, persisted as a strong influence for fully a thousand years, couched and concealed in the vague *ideal* of a "rational explanation," even among those who asserted belief in a free creation and a subsequent salvation by God. [5]

The problem with this model is that it applies only to a fully determined object. The "necessity" that initially characterizes only the structure of the syllogism, or reasoning process, filters through and eventually comes to characterize the object that we are attempting to know *through* this process as well. The drawback, then, with using the model of Euclidean geometry is that it only fits an object that is as fully *determined* and necessary as a geometrical figure. Anything that is "looser" or less necessary *cannot* be studied or adequately known by such an instrument. According to Aristotle, who tried to soften this model, it is precisely the mark of an educated person that he does *not* expect a higher degree of accuracy or precision in an explanation than the subject matter will allow; and all areas of study cannot be expected to live up to a common level of accuracy, and to the mathematical level of rigor in particular (MET 995a 15).

This problem arises in an especially acute form when we attempt to "explain" the production of the physical world which, according to the three religions which recognize cognate scriptures - Jewish, Christian, and Islamic - happened by an act of free will by the deity. How can we "explain" a free act of creation by a *necessary* syllogism? The latter would apply only if all of God's actions followed *necessarily* from his nature, and could be deduced as inevitable consequences of his essence. But this is precisely what we are attempting to *deny,* for otherwise creation would no longer be free. Evidently, then, if we are limited to this paradigm, we can never "explain" freedom, we can only explain it away. And this is exactly what happened. Creation tended for Alfarabi and Avicenna, John Scotus Erigena and Albert the Great, Avincebron and Maimonides, to dissolve into a necessary emanation, following the Neoplatonic pattern; some of these thinkers also got into difficulty with their co-religionists for their apparent departure from religious ortho-doxy. In fact, the recurring danger coming from contact with Greek philosophy for all three of these traditions during the Middle Ages can be described as "rationalism" or "essentialism" - that is, a model of expla-nation aspiring to deduce consequences mechanistically from essences, with every object under discussion, including the deity, strapped onto a "Procrustian bed," and distorted or mutilated until it conforms to this mathematical paradigm of clarity. All three traditions proclaim free creation, but in practice thinkers in all three traditions were tempted to sacrifice this doctrine on the altar of "knowledge," to have faith eclipsed and eventually *replaced* by knowledge.

Nor did the intimidating influence of this model die out with the Middle Ages. Whenever thinkers have felt themselves living in the dispensation of a hostile or untrustworthy deity, a world which could be deceiving us or playing tricks upon us, there is a natural tendency to fall back upon this rationalist paradigm as the best defense, as the safest course for arranging our expectations; it may not be able to explain everything, but on the other hand it will never lead us into error. If we restrict ourselves to its predictions, we cannot go wrong. This mentality would tend to allow "free creation" only as a concession to the pictorial imagination of the masses; the elite have seen the impossibility of free creation, and have in fact cut out or burned away the need for it in their psyches. We find this mentality and strategy repeated later in Spinoza, when the mathematical paradigm of explanation has again risen to prominence at the beginning of the modern Enlightenment. Spinoza feels that the truly "enlightened" philosopher, the one who has risen to an Aristotelian contemplative (and resigned) love of the deity, will have recognized that free will is impossible for God, and as a consequence will have caused his *desire* for free will to be extracted or burned away. God is "determined" by his own essence, whereas you and I are determined by causes outside ourselves (**Ethics**, Pt. I, Def. VII). Further, Spinoza writes that "He who truly loves God would never desire that God love him in return" (Pt. V, prop. 19). Although painful in itself, cutting away or cauterizing our desire for such a relationship is the best, the least painful way to escape persisting and unrelenting frustration. This goes directly against the biblical message of all three faiths.

Plotinus would not have felt too unfamiliar in the Spinozistic philosophy; the two inhabit a similar psychological landscape. Both philosophies are best understood as manuals for *personal salvation,* understood as the escape from illusion and return to the deity; both assume that we find ourselves in a basically hostile or untrustworthy realm of appearances, and must make the clarification of our ideas and the return to God (two descriptions of the same process) by *ourselves,* for God can take no step towards us, nor do anything directly to relieve our condition. In both philosophies, how we emerged or "fell" from our divine origin into this condition of alienation remains a puzzle - more than that, a sorrowful mystery. For both, once you recognize that God cannot love *anyone* (but himself), this insight should lead you to stop desiring it, should turn your "dark passions" into a "clear resignation." For Spinoza, this awareness or knowledge automatically clarifies, corrects, and *changes* our passions, it transforms our "unclear" ideas into "clear" ideas, we arrive at a resigned love of the deity and a reconciliation to our condition. But a similar eradication of desire is called for in the Aristotelian philosopher, once he sees that God is aloof and must necessarily remain so. If the philosopher is to salvage any happiness, or the pleasure which accompanies excellent activity, he must somehow remove or cauterize his desire for an explanation of the production of the world, because he now recognizes that, in principle, there can be no such explanation. He will do this, if only out of enlightened self-interest, for he also recognizes that if he does not eradicate this desire, it will remain perpetually frustrated.

The Christian philosophers (apart from Scotus Erigena and Albert the Great) were more careful than Avicenna and Avincebron at resisting the Neoplatonic model of the production of the world through a necessary emanation, but their initial programs of explanation are implicitly the same, in the sense of as naively or enthusiastically rationalist in intention and ideal. After all, they argue, the God of faith is also the God of nature. The same God who calls us to *believe,* is the God who has made the faculty of *reason;* and since he is a benign deity, he would not give us an instrument which is untrustworthy, or which must be essentially frustrated. More specifically, for Augustine the characteristics of all truth (natural or revealed), in contrast to opinion, are its universality and necessity; further, both have a common source in Christ as the interior teacher. In the Greek tradition from Plato onwards, "faith" or "opinion" (*"PISTIS"* - *"DOXA"*) had traditionally been *subordinated* to knowledge or science (*"EPISTEME"*) as an inferior brand of cognitive activity.[6] The God who redeems the world is also the God who made it in the first place; faith and reason are concerned with the same object, and hence they cannot be opposed. Gregory of Nyssa in the fourth century was the first who tried to find rational arguments for all the teachings of the Church, including the mysteries of the Trinity and the Incarnation. This rationalist tendency reaches its culmination in the eleventh century, when Anselm of Canterbury, the "second Augustine," described his situation as "faith seeking understanding," and himself, like Augustine, as seeking the "necessary reasons" behind these same mysteries; other thinkers, while recognizing that faith must *precede* understanding, took as their goal to go as far as they could in *replacing* faith with reason; and no one knew how far, in advance, this project might succeed. This is the tendency of the programs of Boethius, Abelard, Richard of St. Victor, and (more clandestinely perhaps, but also more consistently) Siger of Brabant.[7] The so-called "ontological" proof of God's existence by Anselm (perhaps better called the "ideational" proof, since it treats existence as a logical property of essence, and tries to deduce it from essence) is a striking example of the power which this rationalist paradigm exercised over these Christian thinkers.

The first and most serious casualty of the uncritical acceptance of this paradigm is the relation between essence and existence in the ontological makeup of an entity. A sensitivity to being as a real aspect of a thing not reducible to its form (or bare possibility) had been spreading in Western thought at least since the time of Aristotle; but no adequate way had been found to handle it, or to relate it to essence. "Existence" was in the uncomfortable position of being "half-born"; it was half in and half out. There was no going back, and yet the way ahead was not clear. It was recognized, and so its reality could no longer honestly be denied; but as yet no way had been found to relate it adequately to the *other* aspect of a thing, its essence or form.

Aristotle had begun by objecting to the possibility of a Platonic "master science" that would cover the entire range of being (which the political ruler should study), on the grounds that the term "being" (or the verb "is") is not an ultimate *genus* that marks off a determinate sector of reality (which you must have to establish an Aristotelian science). On the contrary, the term "being" is *not* used univocally in ordinary speech, so that we cannot form a single definition of it, or mark off clearly the area to be studied. He eventually came to feel, however, that the equivocation in the way "being" is used is not radical, that the ways are tied together by reference to one primary usage or meaning (a usage which Thomas would later call "analogous" predication, here "equivocation by reference to one thing"), and that a "science" of metaphysics, or "being *qua* being," a science in a modified or looser sense, is finally possible. (Aristotle had already relaxed the strict Platonic limitations of science from univocal and necessary objects when he allowed for a theoretical science of *physics*, or moving substances.) This science of metaphysics would correspond to Plato's "master science," which the philosopher-king must study.[8]

Confidence in the regularity and partial (or finite) substantiality of the physical world (the basis for analogy) began to erode, however, during the Hellenistic era, and the mathematical or Platonic model rose again in favor; "existence," although recognized and thematized, was flattened out and reduced to a univocal concept, as "common being." Existence was no longer an analogical property dispersed variously throughout the "great chain of Being," but now only a logical trait, the same for all beings which happen to enjoy present reality, and which marks them off as distinct from merely *possible* beings. However, this became a puzzling trait; difficulties were encountered in articulating its precise relation to essence. It was certainly different from essence (since it was different from "possible being"), but its relationship to essence was not clear. On the one hand, it seems difficult to *deny* it, once it was pointed out; it seemed an incontestably real or empirical property of things. There was no going back now, no legitimate way to dispute or deny its reality. But on the other hand, it was difficult to give a definite content (or definition) to existence, as one could with all other empirical traits. By comparison, it seems transparent, *without* a character of its own; on the-contrary, it seems to slip through one's fingers like water. To borrow an image from the Czech novelist Milan Kundera, it was difficult to give adequate conceptual expression to the empirical experience of the "unbearable lightness of being"; like an atmosphere, it is present all around us, irritating in that, on the one hand it cannot be dismissed out of hand or ignored, yet also lacking a definite geographic location, any recognizable heft or concentrated viscosity by which it can be grasped, and thus eluding all conceptual attempts to capture it. The temptation is to force a contraction, to reduce being to something more concrete which we *can* grasp - possibly matter, or the Forms: to make it into either an essence or an accident (or logical corollary) of essence. Anselm tried to deduce existence, in armchair fashion, as a property of the divine perfection; some, after recognizing it as real, simply conceded defeat and placed it next to essence as an autonomous character set in accidental juxtaposition in those things which, unlike God, are only "possible" or contingent, and not necessary. Almost all found it maddening to work with, and not a few, like Berkeley and Kant later, eventually threw up their hands and dismissed the term as ultimately meaningless, the most abstract and least informative of all ideas. In a desperate and dramatic reversal of Anselm's celebrated "ontological" argument (which he named), Kant will claim that existence is not a meaningful trait at all, let alone a "perfection," that it adds nothing to an idea of which it is predicated.[9] Here the frustration seems to have boiled over to the point where thinkers are tempted to define the problem away, rather than admit that they simply cannot solve it. Thomas Aquinas will resist this mathematical distortion of the problem by distinguishing the analogous act of existence, grasped by an act of *judgment,* from the vacuous idea of "common being," grasped as the last act of *abstraction,* to which we are eventually led by the flat term "being," and language's natural tendency towards univocal understanding. This strategy apparently was too subtle or difficult for many later thinkers. During the "mental housecleaning" of the eighteenth-century Enlightenment, "existence" becomes the most notorious and reviled, indeed, the chief offender in a long list of "unclear ideas" (including substance, matter, eventually cause-and-effect, and even free will) to be tossed out because they do not live up to a preconceived rationalist and univocal model of "clarity and distinctness."

Just as a sensitivity to existence is related internally to the doctrine of the free creation of the world, as was mentioned in the last chapter, so a *difficulty* in handling the trait of existence is symptomatic of or bespeaks a correlative difficulty in explaining the production (and true independence) of the world. Avicenna and Avincebron, for example, following the Middle Platonists, put the Platonic "Forms" as ideas in the mind of God, and they have God "create" them as his necessary effects. They thus have only a nominal doctrine of creation; in effect they tend to dissolve "creation" into a necessary emanation from the godhead. Also, we creatures lose our independence; we are totally determined effects and, indeed, only parts of God, late consequences of his self-unfolding. A strong insistence on the doctrine of divine *providence* (understood as predestination) - fate, or *"KISMET"* - led in practice to an evaporation of the belief in human freedom. Jewish and Muslim thinkers typically had a weak sense of the "will" as a faculty distinct from the intellect; it was Augustine who explicitly separated it off for the Latin Christians, in his discussion of the origin of evil. By the other thinkers, willing is viewed typically as the decision-making act of the intellect, rather than as the act of a distinct faculty.[10] From this perspective, the *clarity* of an idea virtually decides the issue of its acceptance automatically: an idea that is clear enough *inevitably* obliges and compels our assent. This view of the mind was implicitly accepted by the modern Enlightenment as well; and the tendency of this way of conceiving the mind is unmistakably to threaten freedom. Similarly, the Islamic philosophers distinguish existence from essence in the makeup of a thing, but they tended to make existence either totally independent of essence, an *accident* of essence, or alternatively to subordinate it as a necessary *consequence* of essence (and on occasion both, as in Avicenna). However, neither of these solutions seems to be an adequate way of relating existence to essence, or of doing justice to our experience of enjoying at least a relative autonomy and self-directedness *vis. a vis.* both God and the world around us.

It was left to Thomas Aquinas to build on Plotinus and to mobilize the Aristotelian device of act and potency to illuminate this relationship. Existence is the act of God, in itself best conceived as infinite or unbounded. In creatures, *essence* and existence are distinct; indeed, this is the badge of their derivativeness or creaturehood. Further, essence now stands in a limiting or potential relation to the (infinite) act of existence; where for Aristotle *form* actualizes matter, now essence (form and matter together) is in a further dependent (or potential) relationship to an underlying and infinite "act" of existence, in which it participates. A tripartite structure replaces the previous dualistic analysis. Creatures can only be actualized or participate in the infinite act of existence which is God to the extent that their essences will allow. Neither essence nor (finite) act of existence can exist apart from the other; they are mutually-referential and correlative principles, not distinct things. This relationship is more intimate than the accidental juxtaposition Avicenna had envisaged, but it also preserves the distinctness of the two principles from evaporating into either a logical identity or a rigid deduction of one from the other, as the only two options available under the rationalist model. For these reasons it seems a more satisfying expression of the relationship between essence and existence than these earlier thinkers had achieved.

But our explanation for the production of the world is still not adequate or complete. For what leads God to create the potentialities of essence and then to bestow individual "acts" of existence? What leads God to actualize *some* essences over others, or for that matter, why should God actualize *any* essences at all?

NOTES

1 These two forms of perfection correspond, of course, to the two antithetical meanings A.O.Lovejoy found jostling beneath the surface of the word "God," in his classic work The **Great Chain of Being** (Harvard Univ. Pr., Cambridge, reprint 1961). Lovejoy writes: "The one was the Absolute of otherworldliness - self-sufficient, out of time, alien to the categories of ordinary thought and experience, needing no world of lesser beings to supplement or enhance his own eternal self-contained perfection. The other was a God who emphatically was not self-sufficient nor, in any philosophical sense, "absolute"; one whose essential nature required the existence of other beings, and not of one kind only, but of all kinds which could find a place in the descending scale of the possibilities of reality - a God whose prime attribute was generativeness, whose manifestation was to be found in the diversity of creatures and therefore in the temporal order and the manifold spectacle of nature's processes." ibid., p. 315.

2 This theory has left its trace in the Christian scriptures. As St. Paul writes in his second letter to the Corinthians: "All of us, gazing on the Lord's glory with unveiled faces, are being transformed from glory to glory into his very image by the Lord who is Spirit." And the author of the first letter of John writes:

> Dearly beloved, we are God's children now;
> what we shall later be has not yet come to light.
> We know that when it comes to light we shall be like him,
> for we shall see him as he is. 1 John 3:2

3 The philosophical criticism of "anthropomorphisms" may go beyond a simple objection to the improprieties and vulgarities attributed to the gods in various popular mythic collections. In **Tragedy and Philosophy** (Princeton Univ. Pr., 1968), Walter Kaufmann puts forward the provocative suggestion that it was the direction Greek tragedy was taking, from Aesychylus through Sophocles to Euripides, that gave rise to philosophy, by way of *reaction*. Specifically, this movement in tragedy is from comparative *faith* in reason and the goodness of the gods, to a progressively darker vision both of the gods and of the (potential) nobility of man (pp. 296-301). Paul Ricoeur, in **The Symbolism of Evil** (Beacon Pr., Boston, 1967) similarly suggests that tragedy presents us with an "unthinkable" theology, that is, a theology which indicts the gods for what evil there is in the world (p. 225). Kaufmann attributes to the first philosophers - Plato and Aristotle - a failure of nerve, an inability to deal with or accept this blasphemous theology. Plato explicitly sets out three laws which he would force the poets to observe in his ideal "republic," the chief of which is that the gods are responsible only for what is good (and the second of which is that the gods do not change). Kaufmann further indicts Aristotle of being capable, in his **Poetics**, of only a "formalistic" analysis of the power of tragedy, of being unable to discuss the true source of the distinctively tragic pleasure: that it gives us the occasion to voice our rebellion against the orthodox piety Plato had pronounced, the chance to give expression to the "unthinkable possibility," the "black" theology which Ricoeur has described, without guilt or fear of punishment - a hidden suspicion and intellectual passion which finds nowhere else a socially acceptable occasion to come to the surface.

Thus, whether based on conviction or weakness, philosophy apparently felt that the direction in which the imaginative accounts of the gods were going had to be criticized and corrected.

4   In contemporary Narrative Theology, or "Theology of Story," this ancient problematic is provocatively reversed. Here the scriptural accounts are appreciated not as only "story," but as the *best* story. In this modern problematic, all accounts (including those purportedly "scientific") are subsumed within the encompassing category of story; the operative contrast is not between a "scientific account" that would somehow be "non-story," but rather between different *levels* of "story" that are more or less complete or adequate to disclose the profundity and richness of our situation. In this modern way of approaching explanation, we never get outside the category of "story"; rather we can merely rank different accounts as more or less adequate or complete *within* the category of "story." The standards of rigor are internal; there is no external set of conventions to which they must conform. Metaphor and anthropomorphism are no longer objectionable *per se,* as lapses into myth, nor are "philosophic accounts" automatically valued higher; rather, both are tested and evaluated as to how well they are able to disclose the richness of our mature experience, to open up possibilities of self-understanding and development. There is not necessarily a bias *against* the philosophical conventions; rather, they now make their claims felt as elements *within* our experience, rather than as a set of rules external to this experience to which our accounts must nonetheless conform. In practice, then, the two procedures may result in similar accounts.

5   Jewish and Moslem philosophy during the Middle Ages was primarily taken up with reconciling the apparent discrepancies between the "revelation" of the prophets and the "wisdom" of Greek (esp. Neoplatonic) philosophy. There were apparent contradictions on such matters as the eternity of the world, the extent of divine providence (since the philosophical God is aloof and cannot be concerned with beings below him), and the resurrection of the body. In Avicenna, Averroes, and Maimonides, a "solution" emerges which reconciles the two by distinctly subordinating faith to wisdom. For all three thinkers, the human spirit rises to intellectual knowledge only by illumination from a single, separate "Agent Intellect," the last of ten

"intelligences" which move the heavenly spheres, and which are produced necessarily as successive emanations from the "One" or the
"Unmoved Mover." (For Maimonides, these ten intelligences are the
philosophical analogues of scripture's angels.) For all three, the gift
of prophecy is a special power to adapt purely "intelligible truths" to
imaginative symbols, thereby making these truths accessible to the
masses. For most people, the religious approach to truth is best;
however, the (few) erudite who are capable of a philosophical
understanding are free to "interpret" these same scriptural texts to
uncover the purely intelligible truth hidden behind the veil of symbol
and allegory. Both religion and philosophy, they insist, point toward
the same truth; but the religious texts present this truth in symbolical
form; only the philosopher sees the truth as it is. For Maimonides
prophecy is susceptible to many grades, and is most fully realized in
Moses. Knowledge through union with the Agent Intellect is identified with the "eternal life" promised by scripture. The perfection of
philosophical knowledge automatically brings with it moral perfection and immortality. As stated, an assimilation of religion to
philosophy seems to have taken place, but with it a distinct subordi-
nation of "faith" to "reason," as different but not equivalent means of
grasping the same "truth."

6   The transition and re-evaluation of "belief" as related to "knowledge," from Plato to late Neoplatonism, is described by J.M. Rist,
Plotinus: the Road to Reality, ch. 17.

7   This interpretation is presented in more detail by Josef Pieper,
Scholasticism, Pantheon Bks., N.Y., 1960, ch. XI. In this regard,
even Thomas Aquinas has to be careful. Thomas holds that the same
truths cannot be both believed and known (**De Veritate** 4.14, 9).
Because some apparent truths of "faith" can also be demonstrated
(e.g., the existence and unity of God), Thomas chooses to call them,
not truths of faith, but rather "preambles" to faith. Following
scripture, Thomas holds that we are saved by our "faith," and *not* by
our knowledge; thus he holds that there are (fortunately) some truths
which can *only* be believed, and not demonstrated (e.g., the existence
of God as a trinity). See F. Copleston, **A History of Philosophy**, Vol.
2, Pt. II, ch. 32 (Image Bks., N.Y., 1962, p. 33).

8   This reconstruction of the evolution of Aristotle's thinking on the possibility of a science of "being *qua* being" is presented by G.E.L. Owen in "Logic and Metaphysics in some earlier works of Aristotle," **Aristotle and Plato in the Mid-Fourth Century**, During & Owen eds., Goteborg, Sweden, 1960, pp. 178-9. See also W.D. Ross, "The Development of Aristotle's Thought," in **Articles on Aristotle: 1 Science**, Duckworth, London, 1975, pp. 1-14.

9   See I. Kant, **Critique of Pure Reason**, A 599, B 627.

10   See Hyman & Walsh, **Philosophy in the Middle Ages**, Hackett Pub. Co., Indianapolis, 1974, p. 5.

CHAPTER FIVE

THE GREEK CONVENTION OF DIVINE SELF-LOVE; VINDICATION THROUGH INTENSIFICATION

The Parmenidean convention of divine perfection or self-comple-tion, though "expanded" to allow for productivity, was not discarded or overthrown by the medieval scholastics; it survived, and as the period progressed it emerged to reassert its legitimate claims in a powerful and interesting form. This "return of the repressed," so to speak, of the doctrine of God's necessary self-love (a doctrine deeper than and inde-pendent [as regards its truth] of the previously discussed "unchangeable-ness" of God), and its reintegration with the distinctive Christian "good news" of the surprising and almost embarrassing divine condescension and suffering on man's behalf, represents one of the most daring and impressive achievements of late scholastic thought, for it brought to a resolution the outstanding dilemma which had simultaneously bedeviled and propelled Western speculation from the time of its discovery as the inherent and apparently irreparable *lacuna* within Greek philosophy.

Although he may be productive, God cannot be said to "move" for just any odd reason. As Hamlet puts it:

> *Rightly to be great*
> *Is not to stir without great argument.*
>
> Act IV, sc. v

As Aristotle goes to some pains to observe, God has no potentiality, he needs nothing. If he does something (such as the free production of a world), then it must be for a sufficient motive. Anything *less* than the proper motivation would not be adequate to rouse God from his position of absolute rest and self-completeness. For the Greeks, love must be proportional to the worth of an object; to love an object (or a person) *beyond* its merits is not a virtue but a vice. (This is perhaps most graphically presented in Aristotle's discussion of the friendship between unequals in Bk. 8 of the **Nicomachean Ethics**. Here [and contrary to John the Evangelist] he explicitly states that God and men *cannot* be friends.[1] The distance between the two is too great; further, God can get nothing from this relationship that he desires or that would be commen-

101

surate with his greatness. Similarly in the **Symposium,** Socrates posits the need for such intermediary "spirits" as Love, for "the divine will not mingle directly with the human, and it is only through the mediation of the spirit world that man can have any intercourse, whether waking of sleeping, with the gods." 203a) For God to move for anything *less* than the proper motivation would be inappropriate, and unbecoming to his nature. We can say further that, if it is true that Greek thought changed under the influence of the doctrine of free creation, it is equally true that Christian thought evolved as a result of the influence of the Greek doctrine of God's self-sufficiency and his necessary self-preoccupation. In particular, the basis for the Greek objection to the Christian doctrine of the Incarnation - the belief that God could actually take an interest in creatures outside and below himself - reemerges as the Middle Ages progress, makes its "bite" or claim to truth felt, and receives grudgingly its proper acknowledgment and respect. These latter forces propel the program to construct an adequate explanation of the world to one final stage in its development.

From the above considerations we can see that a complete account of the *existence* of the physical world leads naturally to a question of God's *motivation* in producing a world, that is (as we saw at the end of the third chapter), the fact of creation seems to require for its adequate explanation a consideration of "salvation" (understood as God's interest in engaging in a relationship with beings other than himself). In discussing creation, Thomas Aquinas, for instance, never attempts to give a detailed "nuts and bolts" account of how God does it. He expands Aristotle's analysis of the makeup of a moving substance from a dualistic (form/matter) to a tripartite description (essence is now potential to a distinct and deeper act of existence; essence itself is made up of both form and matter); but this is all done by reasoning *backwards* from the *fact* of moving substances to the *conditions* for such. Thomas never attempts to go in the *opposite* direction, or to tell us how God goes about composing substances. The most he can give us, and the *only* thing he apparently thinks is *essential* or needed in fashioning an adequate explanation of the world, is to supply a *motivation* that would make God's act of creation both free and rational, but which would still respect the Parmenidean convention of divine self-completeness. As stated, God cannot move out of himself for just any odd reason; that would be a "free" act, but it would no longer be rational. Nor can lower substances be merely a necessary consequence of the divine nature. That would make the production of the world *rational,* but it would no longer be free. Thomas will take up the device he receives from the Middle Platonists of creatures existing as ideas in the mind of God; but he will nuance it in such a way as to save both the self-sufficiency of God and the free production of the world. To do this, Thomas must upgrade and recast the Greek conception of perfection, while remaining sensitive to the Parmenidean restriction. Thomas writes:

> ... Some things are both agent and patient at the same time; these are imperfect agents, and to these it belongs to intend, even in acting, the acquisition of something. But it does not belong to the First Agent, Who is agent only, to act for the acquisition of some end: He intends only to communicate His perfection, which is His goodness; while every creature intends to acquire its own perfection, which is the likeness of the divine perfection and goodness. **Summa Theologiae** I, 44, 4

It is a delicate balancing act; Thomas is obviously walking a tightrope. But, as with his solution to the essence-existence relationship, he has found an interesting new approach to the problem.

We can be said to be present as ideas in the divine mind, says Thomas, but these ideas are not necessary effects of the divine nature. God, as self-subsistent and omniscient, is necessarily aware of all the *outside* finite possibilities by which his greatness can be imitated, and from whose perspectives it may be appreciated. *We* are these outside viewpoints, possible rather than necessary ideas, which God may choose to bring into existence or not.[2] God does not *need* these outside reflections, nor are they necessary parts of his own nature. But still, if his nature is (as Plato says) "the Good," or goodness itself, then it is not unfitting (though not required by) this nature that God should elect to bring at least *some* of these outside possibilities into existence. God's desire to *share* his goodness with beings other than himself *could* provide a motivation both sufficient and appropriate to lead him *outside* himself, to the production of the world of "nature." This leads Thomas (following Augustine and Bonaventure) to his provocative *expansion* of the Parmenidean criterion of perfection, even while conforming to its insistence upon the divine self-sufficiency:

> Natural things have a natural inclination not only towards their own proper good, to acquire it if not possessed, and, if possessed, to rest therein; but also to diffuse their own good among others as far as possible. Hence we see that every agent, in so far as it is perfect and

in act, produces its like...Hence, if natural things, in so far as they are perfect, communicate their good to others, much more does it pertain to the divine will to communicate by likeness its own good to others as much as possible. Thus, then, He wills both Himself to be, and other things to be; but Himself as the end, and other things as ordained to that end, inasmuch as it befits the divine goodness that other things should be partakers therein. **S.T.** I, 19, 2

Friendship cannot exist except towards rational creatures, who are capable of returning love and of communicating with one another ...Strictly speaking, therefore, God does not love irrational creatures with the love of friendship. **S.T.** I, 20, 2, reply to obj. 3

Thus, as far as he can (for like produces like), God will create another "god," the closest approximation to himself. There is a limit as to how far this can be achieved, when using creatures; but this still seems the best (or least inadequate) description we can give of God's project. God wants to share himself as fully as possible with some one else, to bring about the closest possible imitation of and communion with himself. Anything less than the best that creatures can achieve in this regard would not be worthy of his attention or be sufficient to "move" him to creation in the first place (although creation, as Fr. Copleston has explained, is not technically a "motion"). "Reason" seems to be a crucial property, if even a remote, but still acceptable, approximation is to take place, for only creatures which have it are capable of appreciating God and recognizing his greatness. It is thus in the knowing faculty (as well as in charity) that the greatest sharing in God's greatness takes place. Creatures without reason would not be capable of prompting God to the act of creation. They are thus willed now not for their own sake, but as making possible those that *are* capable of sustaining this kind of relationship.

"Salvation," or communion (friendship) with God, is thus a motive both sufficient and necessary to *explain* creation. But how shall we understand this "goodness" of God? We return here to the Greek objection and the Parmenidean convention: God must certainly love the highest object around; but is it appropriate for him to love beings *lower* than himself?

Thomas admits that God loves better things more (**S.T.** I, 20, 4); he undercuts or dissolves part of this dilemma by his striking suggestion that God's knowledge and will are *constitutive* of the goodness of their objects, rather than being merely responsive to (and dependent upon) them, as is the case with creatures (**S.T.** I, 20, 2). We are as "good" as God makes us (or, expressed differently, he wants to make us as good as we can be. His will is not a *limit* on how good we can be [if anything, *we* limit how good God can make us], even if it is the ultimate cause). Thus one basis for the opposition falls away, as God does not really expect to get something he does not already possess from the objects he knows and loves. But a basis for the opposition remains, for which creatures would it be appropriate for God to bring into existence, granted that he knows them all (as possible imitations of himself)? Obviously, ones that can receive and imitate him most adequately, that is, ones that can appreciate his greatness and reflect it back, ones to whom the depth and extent of his goodness can be most fully revealed. Absolutely speaking, Thomas says that angels are of a higher nature than men; but the human nature of *Christ* is of a higher nature even than the angels (because it is suited to be united to the godhead) - indeed it is worth more than all created existence (**S.T.** I, 20, 4, replies to obj. 1 & 2). Thomas invokes original sin to explain this apparent exception God makes in creating the human nature of Christ, without which his love for mankind would constitute a deviation from the Parmenidean or Aristotelian convention: "God did not assume human nature because, absolutely speaking, He loved man more, but because the needs of man were greater; just as the master of a house may give some costly delicacy to a sick servant, that he does not give to his own son who is well." (ibid.).

None of the Christian thinkers will seriously question the Aristotelian proposition that God is most properly taken up with *himself*. But how does one reconcile this description with the Christian announcement of the almost embarrassing and scandalous intervention, suffering, and death of the "Son of God" on man's behalf? As the eighth psalm puts it:

What is man that you should keep him in mind,
mortal man that you care for him?

Expressed bluntly, are human beings worth this? Doesn't this divine "condescension," self-sacrifice, and self-expenditure on man's behalf seem almost garishly extravagant, inappropriate, and out of scale? The idea that a God should sacrifice himself for even his rational creatures seems strangely out of proportion and unseemly, the result, perhaps, of a morbid, out-of-control wishful thinking or narcissistic self-flattery on man's part. For the Greeks, it is laughable that a God should even *live*

among men, much less *die* for them (as St. Paul found out when he tried
to preach in Athens). And it is certainly anti-Aristotelian: it is not simply
that God *does* not do this; rather, he *can* not do it, it would be ruled out
in principle. How, then, can these thinkers announce the Christian gospel
and still retain *anything* of the Aristotelian (or Parmenidean) understanding of God? Or, if they cannot refute the Aristotelian description of God's
activity, how can they retain this description and still preach the Christian
gospel? Are these not two mutually contradictory portraits, and as such
definitively, irremediably opposed?

Using a kind of "intellectual judo," Christian thinkers will find a way
to engineer the potential opposition between these two descriptions of
God into a relationship whereby they mutually tolerate, support, and
indeed almost seem to imply one another. That is, they will not try to deny
or suppress the potentially contrary or subversive Aristotelian account of
the godhead, they will rather reinforce and *intensify* it, but then also direct
it to their own purposes. They will discover a way to use this self-
preoccupation of the deity in such a way that the opposition to God's
interest in other beings, and in particular his intervention on man's behalf,
is dramatically removed. Indeed, they discover that, if his self-love is
strong enough, by a surprising and almost magical transformation, the
latter can be made to appear, not only as no longer problematic, but as
indeed something one might almost expect.

As mentioned, Thomas will declare that God must know all creatures
(at least as possibilities in his own mind) just in knowing himself. In fully
appreciating his own glory or nature, he must know how this glory would
appear from various "outside" perspectives; thus, the knowledge of one
simultaneously involves the knowledge of the other. They are not
opposed. As we will see, Thomas transfers the Plotinian solution of the
problem of God's knowledge of other beings to the deeper problem of his
mysterious *love* of other beings, which is the true difficulty in the project
of generating an adequate account for the production of the world. As
before, the solution is arrived at through a form of "intellectual judo"; that
is, in not running *away* from a force which appears threatening and
dangerous, but precisely the reverse, in turning to face it directly,
intensifying it, and finding therein, paradoxically, the solution to our
difficulty.

The question is, *which* of these "outside reflections" or viewpoints
will God elect to bring into existence, to move from "possible existence"
to "actual existence"? For that matter, why should God elect to bring *any*

possibility into existence at all? After all, his glory is complete as it is, and will be in no way enhanced by this further recognition. Still, following both philosophical and scriptural indications, God is motivated by goodness or love; and according to Aristotle, this love must be directed at the highest object, which is himself. The Christian thinkers will accept this description; in fact, this natural and proper self-love by God is used by Augustine to explain the procession through the three "persons" in the Trinity. But the key point for later thinkers will be that this divine love for himself, even if it does not *require* progression beyond the Trinity, is certainly compatible with it. God's self-love is not an *obstacle* to his interest in other creatures, it is rather *essential* if the latter is to take place. God's self-love must be of a certain *intensity* in fact, for his interest in creatures to become a serious possibility. The two loves are directly, and not inversely, related. God's self-love is not a danger or rival to his love for creatures; it is rather its essential foundation and necessary precondition. They are not mutually opposed, but rather mutually implicative. If the one is intense, the other will be strong as well; and if the first is weak, the latter will die away proportionately.

In this novel perspective, if God's self-regard is great enough, it will move him further to want his nature to be shared beyond the godhead - with creatures, especially with a creature able to appreciate that glory and reflect it back towards its source. It is important to notice (for this shows Thomas' respect for the Parmenidean or Aristotelian convention) that creation is thus not done exclusively out of an "altruism" on God's part (thereby offending the Greek convention of God's necessary *self*-regard). God wants the praise and recognition he *deserves*. It is not a question of *getting* something he does not already have; but if he is going to create at all, he desires to bring into being the creature best able to enter into a relationship with himself, that is, one who is able to appreciate his glory and reflect it back appropriately. Only such a creature is capable of returning to God an insightful and profound response; only such a creature is thus worthy of moving God out of his rest and perfect self-composure. So at this level, the difference between divine altruism and egoism disappears; God's (proper) love of himself and his love of creatures are not opposed, but rather mutually support one another. His love for *himself* spills over and makes him want to call other beings into existence to appreciate and reflect back his goodness; it also makes him want to share with creatures the greatest thing he has to give them - himself. The two motifs - altruism and egoism - no longer oppose one another, but rather mutually imply and reinforce one another. As Abbot William of Saint Thierry puts it:

> You first loved us so that we might love you - not because you needed our love, but because we could not be what you created us to be, except by loving you. **On the Contemplation of God** (c. 1120)

As motivated by "love," too, this sharing of himself is not simply a mechanistic overflow or emanation from himself, in which God is unconscious or oblivious of the consequences he is necessarily causing - which was the only device Plotinus could invoke to explain the production of the world, since for Plotinus God is *forbidden* from becoming interested in beings other than himself. Now this production requires an act of the *will*. Also, "love" as a motive successfully combines tendency with *freedom;* that is, this sharing cannot be said to be "necessitated" by God's nature, although it is congruent, fitting, or suited to this nature. Thomas writes:

> . . . God wills things other than Himself only for the sake of the end, which is His own goodness; it does not follow that anything else moves his will, except His goodness. So, as He understands things other than Himself by understanding His own essence, so He wills things other than Himself by willing His own goodness. **S.T.** I, 19, 2, reply to obj. 2

God's "goodness" seems to function here as something almost distinct from God, as both source and goal, that is, as both efficient and final cause. God acts "from His goodness" as well as "for His goodness." The ambiguity arises because Thomas is using a distinction which obtains for creatures and is applying it to God, where of course it collapses. Thomas does not mean that God is distinct from his own goodness. But this way of putting it helps to explain - as well as it can be explained - how God can be both self-contained, and also naturally (but freely) productive, or tending to diffuse his goodness - and how these descriptions are not necessarily opposed nor mutually exclusive.

But will any creature do as the recipient of God's love, even the most dull or rudimentary? Here various formulas come into play, and differences arise. For Thomas, *every* level of creation has to come into existence, so that the world *as a whole* is required to express the fullness of the divine perfection.[3] Man is the highest (after the angels), and as such he is essential; but it is the spectrum of creation as a *whole* which adequately expresses the glory of God. Man is distinctive, however, in that he is equipped to appreciate and respond to the greatness of God. Only man can engage in contemplation, as Aristotle would say, or can undertake an intelligent relationship with God; lower creatures cannot do this. Looked at from the other side, God could only share himself fully with a rational creature, so that in a sense all of creation only comes into existence for the sake of the higher creatures. Only they could imitate him at all properly, be receptive and reflect back his goodness; only they consequently could arouse his interest as possible candidates with whom to enter into a relationship. Only they (using the Aristotelian convention) are worthy stimuli to arouse him out of his perfect self-contemplation.

This raises the problem of trying to explain the Christian doctrine of the dramatic "rescue" of man from sin, as carried out through the intervention of God's Son, Jesus Christ. Here again, a possible objection or offense against the Parmenidean convention is turned, by a kind of "intellectual judo," into a triumph by the daring "up-grading" of the divine goodness on the Christian interpretation. God foresaw that man would sin before he created him, and that God would have to send his "Son" to redeem him; but God created man anyway, because only in this way could the extent of God's goodness - the depth and intensity of the love he had to share - be fully and dramatically revealed to his rational creatures. Thus the "condescension" of Christ is not an offense against the Parmenidean convention, but rather the necessary condition if a full communication of God's goodness is to take place.

But even here there is room for two interpretations, and a refinement of the theory with an even closer observance of the Parmenidean stricture. On the one side, Thomas Aquinas holds that the reason for the Incarnation was the sinful condition of man; had mankind never sinned (perhaps an impossible hypothesis, given man's freedom), the Son of God would never have entered the created order to rescue him, for there would have been no need. Thus, says Thomas (following Augustine), the sending of the Son of God, or the creation of the human nature of Jesus Christ was not the original intention and purpose of God from the outset; the decision to take this step was made only *after* (and because) man had fallen (**S.T.** III, 1, 3).

Later thinkers reflected on this view, however, and found it wanting; they called for a new way of viewing the data, one which, interestingly enough, is in even greater conformity with the Parmenidean convention of divine perfection. For in creating man with freedom, they argued, God *must* have known from the outset that he would eventually sin, and that sin would spread its reign so that eventually all mankind would be subject to it. Thus the hypothesis of a sinless humanity was never a serious possibility from the beginning. Although abstractly contingent, then, the Incarnation was *practically* certain or necessary; in no sense could this event be called a surprising, unexpected, or adventitious development. Given his foreknowledge, God was virtually certain from the first moment of creation of the necessity of eventually sending his Son into the world; but if he had known this ahead of time, could the Incarnation, passion, death, and Resurrection of Jesus Christ be said to *not* form part of God's initial intention in creating the world?

The Aristotelian convention (God's primary and necessary self-love or self-regard) asserts itself more strongly in Duns Scotus and Suarez (and many subsequent theologians) than it had in Thomas Aquinas.[4] If God is going to create a world at all, it would *have* to be for the purpose of receiving acknowledgment and praise from the *greatest* being of which creation is capable. To receive praise from any being *less* than this would be to accept a situation in which the world is producing *less* than it is capable of, and this would not be compatible with his nature as God; for a *more* perfect response by the world could be imagined, and God is not deficient in power to achieve the best that is possible. It is thus the *quality* of the appreciation, response, and interaction with another being in which God is primarily interested, not just the quantity; the acknowledgment and praise of this highest creature would mean more to him than that of all the lower creatures combined.

And who is this "perfect creature"? It is here that we see the influence of scriptural theology on these later thinkers, and strangely enough, this influence works to *reinforce* and strengthen the Aristotelian convention, not to fight against it. Through the confluence of these influences, the reasoning and the solution which Thomas had developed to reconcile God's necessary self-love with his dramatic intervention on man's behalf is pushed even farther. Jesus Christ had been defined by the Council of Chalcedon to be "truly God and truly man," one person with two natures. Another way of saying this is that, for the Christian thinker, Jesus Christ combines in his person both the adequate expression of the divine nature in the midst of creation, *and* is also the perfect response to that appearance by a human nature. The latter is Jesus Christ as the pinnacle of creation, or as the perfect creature; and it is *this* being, and this being alone, that could have moved God to produce a world, that *must* have been his intention and guiding purpose from the beginning, the creature that *uniquely* justifies the enterprise of creation. To receive praise and worship from this highest being is the only motive that could have drawn God out of himself.[5] The praise of any creature less than this would have been out of proportion with his majesty and unworthy of his attention. Jesus Christ as the perfect creature is the being who can most deeply and most adequately appreciate the greatness of God in a mutual relationship, and reflect this glory back to God as it ought to be returned. Scotus is surprisingly direct and explicit on this point:

> Therefore, I argue as follows: in the first place God loves himself. Secondly, he loves himself in others and this is most pure and holy love. Thirdly, God wills to be loved by another who can love him perfectly, and here I am referring to the love of someone outside God. Therefore, fourthly, God foresees the union between the Word and the creature Christ who owes him supreme love, even had there never been the Fall. . . In the fifth place, he sees Christ as Mediator coming to suffer and redeem his people of sin. **Reportata Pariesiensia** III, d. 7, 9. 4, n. 5 **Vives** xxiii, 303b

Scotus seems almost to separate the salvific aspect of Christ's activity from his existence as the perfect creature. If God could have created Christ without creating the rest of mankind, he might have done so. The influence of this Aristotelian convention of divine friendship is also clear in such an important later spiritual writer as Francis de Sales. He writes in 1616:

> And since every well-ordered will which determines itself to love several objects equally present, loves better and above all the rest that which is most lovable; it follows that the sovereign Providence, making his eternal purpose and design of all that he could produce, first willed and preferred by excellence the most amicable object of his love, which is our Savior; and then other creatures in order, according as they more or less belong to the service, honor, and glory of him. Thus were all things made for that divine man, who for this cause is called the *FIRST-BORN OF EVERY CREATURE* (Col. 1:15). **Library of St. Francis de Sales**, "Treatise on the Love of God," London, sixth ed., pp. 76-77.

In a sense, these thinkers are merely expanding a point which Thomas also makes, but in a more abridged form. Apparently the Word of God could only be joined to a human (or at least a rational) nature, not to a lower nature:

> Although the Word of God by His Power penetrates all things, conserving all, that is, and supporting all, it is to the intellectual creatures, who can properly enjoy the Word and share with Him, that from a kind of kinship of likeness He can be both more eminently and more ineffably united. **Summa Contra Gentiles** IV, 41, #13

and further:

> God loves Christ not only more than He loves the whole human race, but more than He loves the entire created universe: because He willed for Him the greater good in giving Him "a name that is above all names." . . God loves the human nature assumed by the Word of God in the person of Christ more than He loves all the angels; for that nature is better, esp. on the ground of union with the godhead. **S.T.** I, 20, 4, replies to obj. 1 & 2

Thus it can be said that, for several thinkers who come after Thomas, the world was brought into being to produce Jesus Christ; he is not an adjunct or divine afterthought, nor dependent on mankind's having sinned. Jesus Christ (or rather the second person of the Trinity) was present at creation; but as the perfect creature, he is also the *goal* of creation. The Son of God, as the divine *"Logos,"* is not only the "efficient cause" of the universe; united to a human nature he is also its *final* cause.[6] The distinction between person and nature in Christ was drawn only after the early scriptures were written; there they tend to be not distinguished but run together. As St. Paul writes, in the first role Jesus is "the image of the invisible God, the first-born of all creation, for in him all things were created, in heaven and earth... He is before all things, and in him all things hold together." (Col. 1:15-17) But Christ is also the direction and *telos* of the world, the one whose coming augurs the end-time: "Then comes the end, when he delivers the kingdom to God the Father after destroying every rule and every authority and power... When all things are subjected to him, then the Son himself will also be subjected to him who put all things under him, so that God may be all in all." (1 **Cor.** 15, 22-28) And as the letter to the Hebrews puts it, pushing both images together: "In this, the final age, (God) has spoken to us through his Son, whom he has made heir of all things and through whom he first created the universe. This Son is the reflection of the Father's glory, the exact representation of the Father's being, and he sustains all things by his powerful word. When he had cleansed us from our sins, he took his seat at the right hand of the Majesty in heaven, as far superior to the angels as the name he has inherited is superior to theirs." (1: 2-6)

In this alternative perspective, the Incarnation is not just (or not only) the divine response to our *"FELIX CULPA,"* or "fortunate fall" as Augustine calls it; it rather is the true purpose and reason for creation, and would have happened anyway (in some form), even if man had not sinned. The appearance of the Son of God amidst creation (for communion or friendship with God) was God's goal from the beginning, and not just a sudden and desperate strategy of rescue that God was forced to resort to when man unexpectedly spoiled the original goodness of creation and destroyed God's first plan. It might be too strong to say that the Incarnation would have happened even if man had never fallen, because, theologically speaking, this is probably an impossible hypothesis. It not only *did* not happen, it *could* not have happened. Giving rational creatures the freedom to respond either appropriately or not to himself made the eventual triumph of sin a practical certainty; making rational, free creatures seems to involve, then, the eventual choice to send his Son to rescue them. On the other side, it is also true that God's goodness (in its extent and depth) could only be adequately revealed by sending his Son into the world to rescue a fallen humanity. The two go together, then. God could not will creation without being disposed to will the Incarnation; and perhaps man's "fall" did not spoil God's "first" plan, but on the contrary was the "attractive" element about creation from the beginning, in that it would allow God to manifest his goodness more completely.

More deeply, however, in this latter perspective, the Incarnation conditions, as a motive in the mind of God, the act of creation; Christ as the perfect creature was God's intention from all eternity, and mankind in general only in so far as we are necessary to produce (and are intended eventually to conform to) the Christ. Even now we are "saved" through being incorporated *into* Christ; God loves us insofar as we are aligned *with* Christ (**Ephesians** 1: 3-10). Thus do we become for the first time worthy of his attention, appropriate objects and recipients of his out-sized love. This perhaps moves mankind a bit off-center in the divine attention, but still present as part of the essential surrounding context. This may be a blow to our pride, perhaps, but, as indicated, it is in surprising conformity with the Christian scriptures. Also, it makes God's motivation less objectionable or more satisfying in a philosophical or Aristotelian context: God is essentially self-preoccupied, or preoccupied with the *best*. The *only* motive sufficient and suitable to cause God to move outside himself is to elicit the acknowledgment and praise of the *highest* being of which creation is capable. Anything less would have been unworthy of his attention and an inappropriate object for his concern. (Jerome and Origen thought that God initially did not intend to create men at all. Creation was rather supposed to stop at the level of the "heavenly substances," or angels; man was created only because the angels revolted. This may be viewed as an extreme form of the *"FELIX CULPA"* theory. Thomas Aquinas (and Dante), however, do not share this viewpoint. See **S.T. I**, 61, 3; **Paradiso** 29, 37). Also, it makes the dramatic intervention of God on our behalf appear less excessive and embarrassing; that a god should "die" for mankind was, to a Greek, the absurd limit showing the fundamental error of this new theology which allows God to know or take *notice* of human beings at all. For a Greek, God could not *live* among men, so he manifestly could not suffer or *die* for them. This new motif has the advantage of appearing to correct this imbalance and of restoring God's proper regard for himself. He really did not embark upon the whole enterprise of creation and salvation (only) for us, he did it equally as much for *himself;* for making us, and going through the whole drama of sin and redemption, death and resurrection, was the only way he could produce the *Christ,* both the proper expression of himself, but also, and equally as importantly, the proper *response* to that expression.

It is certainly wrong radically to oppose these two interpretations. The two hypotheses do not really *exclude* one another; rather, again, they seem to tolerate and almost to imply one another. If God's intention in creation truly was to communicate and share his *goodness* to mankind, the *only* way he could make a *full* revelation of the extent of that love (since he knew that man would misuse his freedom), was to give him his freedom anyway - and then take advantage of the dilemma which resulted, to manifest the depth of this goodness. There are limits to how far such a revelation could otherwise take place. Also, going through this step is the only way he could produce the perfect creature, the Christ, the model of a restored and fulfilled humankind. Perhaps both motifs are best seen as specifications of the "divinization" of mankind, which the Greek fathers described as the general plan of creation from the beginning, and the only motif worthy of God; that is, God's intention from the outset was to produce the greatest possible likeness to himself, thus making possible and constituting the most perfect friendship possible with himself. Within the scope of that plan, deploying the two apparently distinct descriptions is analogous to using Cartesian and polar coordinates to plot points on an algebraic graph; they are two different ways of describing substantially the same situation, and have essentially the same content.

However, even if these two interpretations are not opposed, it cannot be denied that they have different emphases, and give a distinct slant to God's project. The one stresses a more traditional interpretation of salvation-history, the other a more philosophical or Aristotelian view of the same. The first is taken from *man's* experience of sin and redemption, the second tries to describe the same process from the point of view of *God's* intention, as desiring relationship with beings other than himself. They are not opposed to each other, even if they perhaps cannot be united under a single higher category. Both are required to express the richness of the situation. The important point for us is that, so far is the Aristotelian convention of divine perfection from being dead that, as we progress through the Middle Ages, the favored interpretation of God's motivation *shifts* from the traditional "two-step" syncopation of sin-and redemption, to the more "Aristotelian" view of God following out a single, consistent plan designed to maximally reveal his goodness and love - by producing both the richest possible display of that love, and also the highest creature to appreciate and reflect back that love. Again, let us stress that the two interpretations do not exclude one another; a choice is made for reasons of preferred emphasis and the appropriate application to our current situation. The one is more helpful for addressing the reality of sin, repentance, and conversion; the other for stimulating the contemplative spirit, a curiosity and awe at the direction God has given to creation, especially to the drama of human history.

So Duns Scotus, in seeming to *violate* the Aristotelian convention of divine perfection (in stressing Jesus Christ as the goal of creation), is actually *conforming* to it at a deeper level. God is so choosy that only the highest that creation is capable of will lure him out of his self-containment. Scotus appears to be flouting the convention deliberately, when he actually ends up *obeying* it in a backhanded sort of way. What he has really done is to find a revolutionary way to re-interpret and to obey this convention - to *intensify* it, and thence to exploit it to his own purposes.

God loves himself *so much,* that he wants to share this love with other beings; and he wants the recognition and love *back* from other beings which he deserves. By this "intellectual judo," Scotus attempts to enlist the force of an apparent enemy, or contrary description of God, and turn this to an advantage, by directing it to his own purpose. The way to overcome the dilemma is not to run away from the apparent danger, but rather to turn to face it, and ingeniously to re-engineer this force in such a way that it ends up supporting one's own position.

On the negative side, one may register one *caveat* to this Scotist strategy: isn't it in danger of succumbing to the same sort of *rationalism* that the Franciscan school had been trying to get away from, and that had been the bane of earlier medieval philosophy and theology? Specifically, two principles seem to be applied in a dogmatic and apodictic way, which prescinds from concrete circumstances, and in such a way that they become questionable. First, the principle that God could only be satisfied with the absolute *best* (in an abstract sense) that creation can produce; isn't it rather the case that God can be (and is often willing to be) satisfied with the best that a particular *concrete* situation can provide (which may fall well below the best conceived in an abstract or ideal sense)? Secondly, in insisting that God must "know ahead of time" that man will sin and that he (God) will consequently have to send his Son into the world, aren't we in danger of not doing justice to the divine freedom (and to human freedom as well)? The objection expressed here is not so much that these principles, as stated, are bluntly wrong, but rather that the issues, as viewed through these categories, are poorly expressed. This seems an incorrect language, and brings with it an unacceptably simple and impoverished way of conceiving a complex situation, one which does not do full justice to the realities of invitation and response, and which thus leads into a false opposition. Without attempting a richer explanation here, we can at least suggest that, for the second point in particular, "process" categories might be more helpful. They are less time- bound, and truer to our experience of the dynamics of free initiative and response. God's offer is the permanent call towards growth and union with himself, an open invitation to follow his divine plan. He knows how he *intends* us to act, but he leaves us genuinely free to follow his invitation, or not. He learns our response as we make it, and *then* he responds in his turn freely to our free act.[7] This way of conceiving the situation safeguards both divine and human freedom, it protects God from the rationalistic strait-jacket through which the divine omniscience seems otherwise to lock both himself and us into a set mode of behavior. This seems more adequate to the data, to the "appearances which must be saved."

It can thus be said that Thomas and Scotus once more revise our paradigm of an "adequate explanation," and in an even more radical or surprising way than before, by compromising and erasing to some extent the line between philosophy and (revealed) theology. For now not only creation, but also salvation is needed to complete our initial project to fashion an adequate explanation for the world. An important contribution from theology is discovered to be needed to complete philosophy and to establish it firmly for the first time in its own order. Philosophy is fully realized *only* when it has made contact with theology; only then is its project complete. This may seem a scandalous outcome for a program which began as the project to "cleanse" the myths; but philosophy is merely being faithful to its deeper program to fashion a satisfactory explanation for the world, as it discovers progressively what is required if this program is to be successfully carried out.

It seems, then, that at the end the two realms are not so distinct after all; the one (philosophy) poses a question which, it discovers, we require some contact with theology to answer. Philosophy stands radically in need of theology and leads naturally into it, if it is to realize its *own* program. To attempt to segregate the two fields is to arrest a single investigation in mid-course, or halfway through. Without being able to go on to theology, philosophy remains a torso of its own projected achievement, an incomplete monument that testifies to the triumph of stubbornness and prejudice over openness and candor. Philosophy that does not lead to theology ends up being simply poor philosophy. Theology is not the perversion of philosophy, but, at least to a certain extent, its natural completion, without which it is and must remain unfinished and unsatisfying in its own order. Theology is not a "second story" built upon an independent and self-sustaining base of philosophy; if anything, theology becomes the basement and (unsuspected) foundation which philosophy later discovers it requires and has been presupposing all along. The project to construct a full or adequate explanation of the physical world does indeed result in a "two story edifice"; but now it is *theology* which constitutes the bottom floor, and philosophy which is surprised to find itself pushed upstairs to become a second story.

The interesting point is that, if scholastic philosophy fills the essential *lacuna* afflicting Greek philosophy, it can also be said that, at its culmination, scholastic philosophy returns and satisfies the strictest convention of Greek philosophy, it adapts itself and answers the chief objection Greek philosophy could lodge against its otherwise very startling, and very un-Greek, message. Parmenides would have been pleased with Scotus, not scandalized by him, and would have recognized him as a spiritual brother - perhaps more so than he would have recognized Augustine or Thomas. What God loves most of all is *himself;* but that is as it should be. Anything *else* would be a scandal. Everything else that God does has to take place within this fundamental context. For the Greeks, love must be *proportional* to the worth of an object; it is wrong to love an object (or a person) beyond its merits. The world begins and ends with God's love for himself; we can merely be *enfolded* within that love. The Christian suggestion is that within the circuit of divine self-love - because God's love and goodness are *strong* enough - there is room for the rest of what we see in the realm of nature and human history to take place. In fact, that is the *only* explanation possible for their existence. If we are not led to this hypothesis by faith in a revelation, we should at least be open to it through the poverty of alternative explanations to account for it. And God's love is so intense or powerful, the announcement is, that the circuit obviously *did* expand to generate the world. The circle did not *have* to expand this far, as an abstract possibility; but it manifestly *did*. We are directed to this speculative hypothesis to take account of the merely natural data or evidence. It is the *intensity* of God's goodness that must here be "factored up," in view of the manifest *reality* of nature; we are thereby indicating or evaluating not specifically the world as good or bad, but simply its *existence* as a non-necessary occurrence. From the fact of creation, as already mentioned, we must reason to the intention of "salvation" or relationship (in a broad sense) as a further necessary precondition and motivation in the mind of God. Any other attempt to "explain" nature simply fails.

God loves himself most of all. But this self-love is not an obstacle to the production of the world or to his love of others, it is rather its necessary presupposition. This is Thomas' and Scotus' discovery. God wants others to love him as he loves himself. Completing the project of philosophy now consists essentially in *gaging* the intensity of that love. We have nothing to fear from God's "egoism" or "narcissism," although Aristotle and the Greeks thought it made creation impossible; on the contrary, the scholastics have discovered, it is compatible with creation and (if it is strong enough) makes creation virtually a certainty, or at least something no longer scandalous. Only if this self-love is strong, is creation possible; and if creation is *actual,* it must be very strong indeed - strong enough at the very least to make *revelation* no longer surprising or a cause for scandal. In fact, the opposite is true, for the absence of revelation would make a relationship with God difficult for most people, and thus creation itself would become ambiguous and for most absurd - at best, a bad joke.

Thus medieval philosophy seems to come full circle and finally at its end to make its accomodation and peace with Greek philosophy, in the sense that it is finally able to reconcile the Christian announcement of a divine initiative with the Parmenidean (or Aristotelian) convention of divine self-sufficiency or perfection. For at its culmination, in the theories of Thomas Aquinas and Duns Scotus, a way is found to move from Aristotle's doctrine of God knowing himself to a doctrine of God *loving* himself as the highest object, a self-love which paradoxically not only does not *exclude* the possibility of a divine initiative beyond himself, but on the contrary makes this adventure entirely fitting and appropriate. The internal dynamic or economy of the godhead is radically changed, indeed revolutionized, by this apparently minor shift of emphasis from divine self-knowledge to divine self-love (or in Thomas' language, to the primacy of *practical* knowledge over speculative knowledge in God [8]); rather than being an obstacle, fresh possibilities of accomodation are dramatically opened up. In the flick of an eyelash, one way of viewing the data "tumbles" into another, and an entirely new viewpoint comes before our eyes; it is the change from the world of Spinoza to the world of Francis of Assisi. In the reality of the triune God, the procession of persons can barely come to a stop within the Trinity; but that at least is a logical, and thus necessary sequence. The intensity of the divine nature as love and goodness, however, pushes on, expands, and leads God to call into existence a world that did not have to be there, a world called into existence to acknowledge a love that also did not have to be as strong as it is. If the most important conclusion of philosophy is the necessity for the divine *existence* (given the world), the central message of Christian revelation is the *contingency* of the divine *goodness* - which nevertheless (we now discover) must also be postulated if we are to give an ultimately satisfying account simply for the existence of the world. Revelation confirms (and completes) what the natural data already points toward and requires.

The broader consequence for philosophy is that the Greek project to explain the natural world cannot come to a stop or a sense of completion with a simple assertion of the *existence* of God (Aristotle), nor can it even come to rest with the stronger assertion of the existence of a God who is productive of the world (Plotinus). Rather, to fully account for the world and to observe consistently the canons of the (never abandoned) Aristotelian convention of divine perfection, the project now sees that it must push on to posit a motivation in God to enter into a positive *relationship* with beings other than himself, specifically with a being capable of appreciating his greatness and reflecting this back. Anything less than this will not be adequate - not just for scriptural reasons, but in order to satisfy strictly Aristotelian or philosophical requirements. Thus, the project to do justice to the apparent autonomy of the natural world demands eventually (and paradoxically) that we relate and subordinate this world to an invisible, transcendent realm from which it was produced; and the effort to explain adequately this production requires further that we subscribe to some theory of "salvation," that is, that God desires to enter into friendship with us, as the divine intention behind this act of production. Reciprocally, the attempt to explain the natural world exhaustively while excluding reference to such a transcendent realm or to such an intention, is moving towards frustration, and has the directly opposite effect of transforming the world into something gratuitous and ultimately absurd.

It thus is not inappropriate or an exaggeration to say that Christian revelation brings to a successful completion the revolution begun by Aristotle - the rendering of God "active" so as to explain the efficient causation of the world - with the surprising discovery that "creation" requires further a theory of "salvation" to become itself complete, that is, if creation is not to become an irrational and capricious "lurch" in the divine substance. Applying itself diligently to complete a merely "natural" explanation, philosophy finds, first, that it must seriously modify its most basic criterion of perfection; as a consequence of this, "revelation" becomes not merely *possible,* but indeed almost required, if creation is not to become irrational. God must definitely have invited us into some relationship with himself, if our situation here is not to fall into a gnostic condition of alienation and despair.[9] Creation must be the first step towards an eventual salvation; until that moment, we are "waiting for the other shoe to fall." The details of this relationship, however, remain incomplete or to be filled in; for that we must await an *actual* revelation, one in *fact,* and not merely in schematic theory. The substantive change in the Greek viewpoint, however, is that any adequate account of the world must discuss a positive *initiative* by God beyond himself; the Greek project must substantially modify and expand the Parmenidean and Aristotelian convention of perfection described above. God must have taken a step *towards* us (he must have *made* us in the first place), and not merely *permit* us to come crawling back towards himself from the *ULTIMA THULE* of our puzzling, mysterious, and sorrowful exile.

Augustine estimed that certain pagan philosophers (chiefly Plotinus) had caught a glimpse of the theological doctrine of the Trinity from afar; Thomas Aquinas differed from him on this, insisting that this doctrine can only be known through revelation. What I have presented here resembles a weaker version of Augustine's view. It suggests that these "pagan" philosophers were working negatively towards, or may even have seen the need for, what is indeed the central and most distinctive tenet of the Judaeo-Christian proclamation - that God *has* taken an initiative towards the world, for the purpose of calling the world into relationship with himself. If so, these thinkers certainly came to this insight for thoroughly this-worldly or "natural" reasons, not because of any respect for a revelation - indeed quite the opposite, *resisting* this hypothesis as a regression into a *pre*-Enlightenment, mythological way of thinking. With some of the patristic thinkers (so impressed were they with the transforming power of knowledge), it is hard to tell whether we are dealing with a religious thinker who has become enlightened, or an enlightened thinker who has become religious, as this hypothesis is eventually accepted as the necessary step if the initial philosophical project of fashioning an adequate explanation of the natural world is to be successfully carried out, that is, if the natural world is to be rescued from becoming an irrational surd. As Irenaeus of Lyons puts it in perhaps his best known passage (c. 180 C.E.):

It is impossible to live without life, and the actualization of life comes from participation in God, while participation in God is to see God and enjoy his goodness. . . The Word became the steward of the Father's grace for the advantage of men, for whose benefit he made such wonderful arrangements. He revealed God to men and presented men to God. . . On the other hand, he revealed God to men and made him visible in many ways to prevent man from being totally separated from God and so cease to be. Life in man is the glory of

God; the life of man is the vision of God. If the revelation of God through creation gives life to all who live upon the earth, much more does the manifestation of the Father through the Word give life to those who see God. **Against Heresies**

Reciprocally, with "free creation" finally accepted, with creation explained (and completed) by salvation, and with the possibility of salvation reconciled with the completeness and self-love of the deity, the final question about the world that needed to be asked has been answered, the last substantive objection from Greek philosophy has received its response; the power of "negativity," as Hegel calls it, that has propelled scholastic philosophy forward has been exhausted; and the Aristotelian project to fashion a scientific and satisfying explanation of the physical world is now (within the purview of its own concerns) completed.

NOTES

1   See Aristotle, **Nicomachean Ethics**, Bk. VIII, ch. 3-10, and line 1159a.

2   Thomas says that God eternally knows his own divine perfection as imitable externally by a plurality of possible creatures. Thomas exploits this device as a way of reconciling the One and the Many, the divine *simplicity* with the apparent need for God to know *many* things. We are justified in talking about "ideas in the mind of God," not as if his knowledge were directed to *many* possible objects distinct from himself, but only in the sense that he knows his own perfection, his own essence, as the *exemplar* of many possible imitations (some of which he may choose to bring into existence). Thus the Aristotelian description of God is preserved. By this loose or "swivel" joint, Thomas can avoid the problems of Avicenna's rather crude solution, and save three important conclusions. First, the divine simplicity is preserved; secondly, a mechanism is supplied by which a plurality of beings is nevertheless known and produced; and lastly, this production remains free rather than necessary. Thomas writes:

> The term *IDEA* does not signify the divine essence as such but in so far as it is the likeness or principle of this or that thing. . . It is not contrary to the simplicity of the divine intellect to

understand many things; but it would be contrary to its simplicity to be informed by a plurality of subjective determinations. **S.T.** Ia, 15, 2, art. 1

Thus, outside objects may be compared to external "mirrors" which catch and throw back the light they receive from the godhead. The higher, conscious creatures are of course capable of reflecting back this glory to a much more powerful degree. The reconciliation with the Aristotelian convention of God's necessary self-love is evident in Thomas' discussion of God's free will:

> About the objects willed by God, note that there is a reality he wills of absolute necessity, yet this is not true of everything real. His will is necessarily related to his own goodness, which is its proper objective. Hence he wills his own goodness necessarily, rather as we cannot but wish our own happiness. For that matter, every ability is similarly related to its proper and principal objective, like sight to color, because to this it tends of its very nature. Now God wills things other than himself in so far as they are set towards his goodness as unto their end. By willing an end we are not bound to will the things that lead to it, unless they are such that it cannot be attained without them. . . Hence, since God's goodness subsists and is complete independently of other things, and they add no fulfillment to him, there is no absolute need for him to will them. However, there is an hypothetical necessity here, for on the supposition that he does will a thing it cannot be unwilled, since his will is immutable. **S.T.** I, 19, 3

3 Thomas writes in **S.T.** I, 47, 1:

> Hence we must say that the distinction and multitude of things come from the intention of the first agent, who is God. For He brought things into being in order that his goodness might be communicated to creatures, and be represented by them; and because his goodness could not be adequately represented by one creature alone, he produced many and diverse creatures, that what was wanting to one in the representation of the divine goodness might be supplied by another. For goodness, which in

God is simple and uniform, in creatures is manifold and divided; and hence the whole universe together participates in the divine goodness more perfectly, and represents it better than any single creature whatever.

4   Other theologians who follow Scotus on this point are St. Bernadine of Siena, St. Laurence of Brindisi, Suarez, Pope Pius XII (while still a cardinal), Karl Rahner, and Teilhard de Chardin. See Eric Doyle, O.F.M., "John Duns Scotus and the Place of Christ," **Clergy Review**, Sept-Nov '72.

5   Lucifer, as the chief of the rebellious angels, would have been the high point of creation before (or apart from) Christ. In this revised "Scotean" perspective, the human nature of Christ, as the "most perfect creature," can be said to be the "new Lucifer," just as St. Paul also describes him as the "new Adam." "Lucifer," in fact, is a non-biblical term for Satan, only used by the Fathers. Interestingly enough, in the two occasions where it appears in the Vulgate (Latin) bible, it refers to *Christ* (the light-bearer), and not to the devil. See Ap. 22: 16 and 2 Pt. 1:19.

6   Christ as the teleological goal of all creation is implicitly contained in the early Christian assertion of Christ as the *"LOGOS"* of God (an understanding which already occurs in the prologue to John's gospel). This elevation of Jesus asserts at least two things. First, the Son of God pre-existed the world. But secondly, Christ also provides the "form" the world should eventually grow into and take on, when it comes to its full developement. The Word was incarnated not only once, in the person of Jesus, but is to be *"re-* incarnated," so to speak, at the end of the world - if and when the world reaches its full development and maturity (and until which, the world is incomplete). But the second, "macroscopic" incarnation can only take place after, and as a consequence of, the first "microscopic" incarnation. Christ has arisen as the first of many brothers and sisters; he is the proleptic anticipation of the life-form that should eventually characterize the world as a whole.

7   The first paragraph of Umberto Eco's well-known novel, **The Name of the Rose**, is a parody of the prologue to John's gospel, and suggests such a gnostic interpretation of our situation:

In the beginning was the Word and the Word was with God, and the Word was God. This was the beginning with God and the duty of every faithful monk would be to repeat every day with chanting humility the one never-changing event whose incontrovertible truth can be asserted. But we see now through a glass darkly, and the truth, before it is revealed to all, face to face, we see in the fragments (alas, how illegible) in the error of the world, so we must spell out its faithful signals even when they seem obscure to us and as if amalgamated with a will wholly bent on evil. Warner Bks., N.Y., 1980, p. 3

G.K. Chesterson has expressed this point more poetically but also more powerfully than I could:

... The more we really appreciate the noble revulsion and re-nunciation of Buddha, the more we see that intellectually it was the converse and almost the contrary of the salvation of the world by Christ. The Christian would escape from the world into the universe; the Buddhist wishes to escape from the universe even more than from the world. One would uncreate himself; the other would return to his Creation: to his Creator. Indeed it was so genuinely the converse of the idea of the Cross as the Tree of Life, that there is some excuse for setting up the two things side by side, as if they were of equal significance. They are in one sense parallel and equal; as a mound and a hollow, as a valley and a hill. It is even true that the truly spiritual and intellectual man sees it as a sort of dilemma; a very hard and terrible choice. There is little else on earth that can compare with these for completeness. And he who will not climb the mountain of Christ does indeed fall into the abyss of Buddha. **Saint Thomas Aquinas**, Sheed & Ward, N.Y., 1954, pp. 134-5

8   Following Aristotle, *practical* reasoning concludes not in a statement, but in an *action*. Aquinas clearly subordinates speculative to practical knowledge in God as creator or the world, which creation is modeled on the relation of an artisan to his product. See **De Veritate** 2.5-2.8. The gradual replacement of the device of divine speculative knowledge by divine practical knowledge to explain the production of the world, through Avicenna and Maimonides to Thomas Aquinas,

is traced by David Burrell in **Knowing the Unknowable God**, Univ. of Notre Dame Pr., Notre Dame, Indiana,1986, chs. 5 & 6.

9   The lines along which the Parmenidean convention of divine perfection might be further modified, in the direction of a process deity and a God who truly *suffers* as a result of our refusal to accept his offer of relationship, are described in the following:

W. Norris Clarke, S.J., "A New Look at the Immutability of God," **God Knowable and Unknowable**, ed. Roth, Fordham U. Pr., N.Y., 1973, pp. 43-72

The Philosophical Approach to God, Wake Forest U. Pr., Winston-Salem N.C., 1979

John H. Wright, S.J., "Divine Knowledge and Human Freedom: the God who Dialogues," **Theological Studies**, 38, 3 (Sept, '77) pp. 450-77
"The Method of Process Theology: An Evaluation," **Communio**, 6 (1979), pp. 38-55

For a more recent discussion, see

Mary F. Rousseau, "Process Thought and Traditional Theism: A Critique," **The Modern Schoolman**, 63, 1 (Nov '85), pp. 45-65

Again, the argument is that these modifications are in the direction of a *greater,* and not less, perfection in God. Thus again the kernel of the argument is that the Parmenidean convention is not broken, just expanded. There is no true violation of the convention, but rather an openness to higher *types* of perfection, in order to handle or explain subsequently discovered exigencies of our experience.

CONCLUSION: RECAPITULATION

The main problem of modern philosophy is to reconcile the determinism of modern science and a generally harsher vision of our situation, with the assumption of freedom and autonomy which underlies the tremendous expansion of thinking, domination, and creativity which has characterized our era since the time of Descartes and Hobbes. Similarly, the problem for ancient philosophy was to reconcile the changelessness and necessary self-love of the deity with the existence of a world that was stubbornly there but was apparently not divine. The existence of the god the Greeks could get to could not generate the world; the existence of the god they needed, they dismissed as a superstition. The fulfillment of the Greek project seemed to require what their tradition forced them to regard as a blasphemy. Aristotle started to show a way out, with his distinction between "activity" and "motion," but was unable to bring this revolution to completion; instead, after a promising start, he too was sucked back into the orbit of the Parmenidean convention of perfection. In its determined resolve to eschew popular myths of divine intervention, the Greek Enlightenment eventually backed itself into a corner, where it was forced to admit that on its assumptions, the world could only be either a necessary appendage to God's nature, or an illusion (or both, as in Plotinus - our higher soul has never really fallen into our body). The encounter with the Christian "good news" thus did not spell doom for Greek philosophy (as the eighteenth-century Enlightenment maintained), but rather served to rescue the Greek project from the dead end and persisting frustration in which it was inextricably stalled. By stressing as fundamental God's movement *towards* a world, Christianity posed directly the problem of how a being which is complete in itself - a substance - could be interested in any beings outside itself, and thus forced Greek philosophy to consider a form of goodness or perfection higher than it had been working with. There is, of course, no necessity for God to be more perfect than that - except our need to explain the existence of the world. Creation is as "scandalous" as salvation from the perspective of traditional Greek philosophy; but salvation (or friendship), once accepted, provides the key or expansion which makes creation for the first time intelligible. They both require the same modification in our idea of God. And reciprocally, creation now almost requires some form of salvation, if the existence of the world is not to become a bad joke. In its final stage of development, Christian philosophy returned to acknowledge the truth contained in the

Greek axiom that God's love must be proportional to its object, and must be directed towards the highest object. If there is to be a creation, God could only be motivated by the best creation has to offer. In an ironical final reconciliation, Jesus Christ in his human nature becomes not only compatible with the philosophical world view, he is almost required or mandated by it, as the only lure that could entice God out of his self-completeness to create a world in the first place.